ManusCrypt

Information security primarily serves these six distinct purposes—authentication, authorization, prevention of data theft, sensitive data safety / privacy, data protection / integrity, non-repudiation. The entire gamut of infosec rests upon cryptography. The author begins as a protagonist to explain that modern cryptography is more suited for machines rather than humans. This is explained through a brief history of ciphers and their evolution into cryptography and its various forms.

The premise is further reinforced by a critical assessment of algorithm-based modern cryptography in the age of emerging technologies like artificial intelligence and blockchain. With simple and lucid examples, the author demonstrates that the hypothetical "man versus machine" scenario is not by chance, but by design. The book doesn't end here like most others that wind up with a sermon on ethics and eventual merging of humans with technology (i.e., singularity).

A very much practicable solution has been presented with a real-world use-case scenario, wherein infosec is designed around the needs, biases, flaws and skills of humans. This innovative approach, as trivial as it may seem to some, has the power to bring about a paradigm shift in the overall strategy of information technology that can change our world for the better.

ManusCrypt

Designed for Mankind—Anthropocentric Information Security

Prashant A Upadhyaya

CRC Press
Taylor & Francis Group
Boca Raton London New York

CRC Press is an imprint of the
Taylor & Francis Group, an **informa** business

Designed cover image: © Shutterstock

First edition published 2025
by CRC Press
2385 NW Executive Center Drive, Suite 320, Boca Raton FL 33431

and by CRC Press
4 Park Square, Milton Park, Abingdon, Oxon, OX14 4RN

CRC Press is an imprint of Taylor & Francis Group, LLC

© 2025 Prashant A Upadhyaya

ISBN: 9781032842400 (hbk)
ISBN: 9781032863641 (pbk)
ISBN: 9781003527220 (ebk)

DOI: 10.1201/9781003527220

Typeset in Sabon
by Apex CoVantage, LLC

To all the past, current and future generations including Gen X, Y, Z, their fathers and grandfathers who have had the opportunity to either see the coming of the digital era or who are living in this era or those who will be witnessing the maturity of this era, as they all have a daunting task of remaining as human as possible.

Contents

Foreword   xv
Preface   xvii
Acknowledgments   xxi
About the Author   xxiii

Introduction   1

  0.0 Mise-en-scène 1
  0.1 Historical Textbooks' Limitations 2
  0.2 Business Consumerism's Limitations 2
  0.3 Importance of a 360-Degree View 3
  0.4 Perspectives, Change Management, and Paradigm Shift 3
     0.4.1 Perspectives and Historical Context 3
     *0.4.2 Change Management and Historical
              Transformations 4*
     0.4.3 Paradigm Shift in Consumerism 4
  0.5 Current State of Affairs 5
     *0.5.1 Human–Machine Interaction (HMI) in Information
              Technology 5*
     *0.5.2 Human Factors Engineering in Information
              Technology 6*
  0.6 Why Should You Read This Book? 7
     0.6.1 Complexity and Learning Curve 7
     0.6.2 Lack of Intuitive Interfaces 7
     0.6.3 Limited Customization 7
     0.6.4 Bias and Fairness Concerns 7
     0.6.5 Ethical Challenges 8
     0.6.6 Invasion of Privacy 8
     0.6.7 Job Displacement 8
     0.6.8 Inflexibility in Problem-Solving 8

0.6.9   *Overreliance on Technology 8*

0.6.10 *Disconnect from Human Interaction 8*

0.7   *Disconnect from Human Interaction 9*

0.7.1   *Description 9*

0.7.2   *Examples 9*

0.7.3   *Concerns 10*

0.8   *The Mechanical Turk 11*

0.9   *Setting the Stage 15*

0.9.1   *The Ubiquitous Presence of Cryptography 15*

0.9.2   *The Balance between Security and Human Privacy 16*

0.9.3   *The Duality of Modern Cryptography 16*

0.9.4   *The Transformation of Communication 17*

0.9.5   *The Human Equation in Encryption 18*

0.10 *Epistle for Bibliophiles 18*

1   **Need for Secrecy and Its History**   **20**

1.1   *Why Secrecy? 20*

1.2   *Secrecy in Communication 22*

1.3   *Types of Secrecy in Modern Communication 23*

1.4   *Evolution of Modern Cryptography 24*

1.4.1   *From Ancient Ciphers to RSA: A Historical Overview 25*

1.4.2   *The Digital Age: Pioneers and Revolutionary Breakthroughs 25*

1.4.3   *Public-Key Cryptography: The Pandora's Box of Data Privacy 26*

1.4.4   *Navigating the Shifting Sands of Encryption Standards 27*

2   **Evolution of Codes, Ciphers, and Cryptography**   **29**

2.1   *Brief History 29*

2.2   *Cryptography around the World 31*

2.2.1   *Ancient Ciphers and Early Cryptography 32*

2.2.2   *Medieval Cryptography 32*

2.2.3   *Cryptography in the Age of Enlightenment 32*

2.2.4   *The Birth of Modern Cryptanalysis 33*

2.2.5   *World War II and Beyond 33*

2.3   *Codes and Ciphers in India 33*

2.3.1   *Ancient India 34*

2.3.2   Medieval India 34

2.3.3   The Mughal Era 34

2.3.4   British Colonial Era 35

2.3.5   Modern India 35

2.3.6   The Atbash Cipher 37

2.3.7   Ardhamagadhi Prakrit Cipher 38

2.3.8   Kutila Samvad 40

2.3.9   Vedic "Katapayadi" Code 41

2.4   Relatability of Ancient Indian Ciphers 42

2.4.1   Shared Principles 42

2.4.2   Algorithmic Complexity 43

2.4.3   Secrecy and Steganography 43

2.4.4   Key Management and Distribution 43

2.5   Comparison of Ancient v/s Modern 43

3   Man v/s. Machine   45

3.1   Perspectives 45

3.1.1   Apparent Reality: Man v/s Machine 48

3.1.2   The Reality: Man v/s (Man + Machine) 48

3.1.3   Ideal Goal: Man + Machine 48

3.2   Apparent Reality: Consumerist Projection 48

3.3   The Reality: Isolation 49

3.3.1   The Dark Side of Convenience: Erosion of Human Interaction 49

3.3.2   Internet Surveillance and Privacy Concerns 50

3.3.3   The Perils of Digital Footprints and Data Breaches 50

3.3.4   Cryptography, Identity, and Digital Personhood 51

3.3.5   The Human Element in Encryption 51

3.4   Ideal Goal: Simple Ethical Machines 52

3.4.1   Balancing Human Needs and Technological Advancements 52

3.4.2   Empowering Humans through Technology 52

3.4.3   Enhancing Efficiency and Productivity 53

3.4.4   Improving Quality of Life 53

3.4.5   Social Impact and Connectivity 53

3.4.6   Ethical Considerations and Human Values 53

3.4.7   Sustainability and Environmental Impact 54

3.4.8   Embracing Ethical Cryptography—Paving the Way for a Harmonious Future 54

3.5   Incongruities with Information Security 55
      3.5.1   Overview of Data Breaches 55
      3.5.2   Lack of Humanistic Design Approach in
              Information Security 61
3.6   Comparative Study of Infosec with Aviation Safety 63

4   Of, for, and by the Machines   66
4.1   Back to Square One 66
      4.1.1   Technological Singularity: A Paradigm Shift in
              Human Civilization 67
      4.1.2   The Promise of Technological Singularity 68
      4.1.3   The Man Versus Machine Scenario 68
      4.1.4   The Path to the Technological Apocalypse 69
4.2   Human Factor in Encryption 70
      4.2.1   Forgotten Trust: The Dependency on Machines 70
      4.2.2   Encryption and Surveillance: Striking the
              Delicate Balance 70
      4.2.3   Cybersecurity and the Human Weakness Factor 71
      4.2.4   The Complex Ethical Landscape 72
4.3   Digital Divide and Information Inequality 72
      4.3.1   Cryptography and Social Stratification 72
      4.3.2   The Unequal Access to Privacy and Security 73
      4.3.3   Economic Disparities and the Encryption Gap 73
      4.3.4   The Role of Education and Awareness 74
      4.3.5   The Social Impact of Encryption Policies 74
4.4   The Moot Question 75

5   Humanistic Design   77
5.1   Prologue 77
5.2   Cryptography and Free Speech 78
      5.2.1   Encryption and Censorship: The Clash of
              Ideals 78
      5.2.2   The Fight for Digital Anonymity: Whistleblowers
              and Activists 78
      5.2.3   The Dilemma of Balancing Free Speech and
              Security 79
      5.2.4   The Impact on Criminal Investigations and
              Justice 80
5.3   Politics of Encryption 81
      5.3.1   National Security and Individual Rights:
              A Never-Ending Tug-of-War 81

5.3.2   Governments, Corporations, and the Power Play of Data Control 81

5.3.3   Cryptocurrency and Financial Surveillance 82

5.3.4   Encryption as a Weapon in Geopolitical Conflicts 82

5.4   Cryptography as a Double-Edged Sword 83

5.4.1   The Encryption Paradox: Crime Versus Privacy 83

5.4.2   Unbreakable Codes and Law Enforcement Challenges 84

5.4.3   The Impact on Criminal Investigations and Justice 85

5.4.4   Balancing Crime Prevention and Privacy Rights 85

5.4.5   Innovative Solutions and Cooperative Efforts 86

5.5   Psychological Implications of Cryptography 86

5.5.1   The Mental Burden of Constant Surveillance 86

5.5.2   Cybersecurity Anxiety: The Fear of Being Hacked 87

5.5.3   The Effects of Living in the Digital Panopticon 87

5.5.4   Intricacies of Trust and Digital Relationships 88

5.6   The Ethical Dilemma 89

5.6.1   The Ethical Tightrope: Balancing Security and Human Values 91

5.6.2   Privacy as a Fundamental Right 91

5.6.3   Encryption and Social Justice 92

5.6.4   Digital Inclusion and Accessibility 92

5.6.5   Responsible Data Practices and Transparency 92

5.6.6   Safeguarding Democracy and Digital Rights 92

5.6.7   Transparency, Accountability, and Responsible Encryption 93

5.7   Finding Common Ground: Ethical Cryptography Principles 93

6   **Anthropocentric Cryptography**   **95**

6.1   From the Heart 95

6.1.1   Difficulty in Controlling Data Breaches 96

6.1.2   Malicious / Bad Actors in Cryptography 98

6.1.3   Need for Change 101

6.2   From the Head 101

7   **ManusCrypt**   **104**

7.1   Human-Centered Cryptography 104

7.1.1   Journey from Natural to Artificial 104

7.1.2   Natural Cryptography 105

7.2   The Solution 106

8   Business Use Case Scenario   109
  8.1   Utility 109
  8.2   Use Case 109
        8.2.1   Collatz Conjecture or Hasse's Algorithm 110
        8.2.2   Python Code for Demonstration of Hasse's
                Algorithm 111
        8.2.3   "Sprouts Game Algorithm" with Worked-out
                Example 116
        8.2.4   Sprouts Game in Python 117
        8.2.5   Python Code for Cryptographic Function Based
                on Steganography 126
        8.2.6   Infinite Generation Function 129
        8.2.7   IGF in Python 129
  8.3   Proof of Concept 132
  8.4   User Experience 133

9   RAM for ManusCrypt   135
  9.1   Custom Source 135
  9.2   Cryptographic Function 137
  9.3   Note 140

10 Architectural Appraisal   141
  10.1 Overview of Solution 141
        10.1.1 N-Tier Architecture 141
  10.2 Utilizing Emerging Technologies 143

11 Paradigm Shift   145
  11.1 Future of Cryptography 145
        11.1.1 Quantum Cryptography: A New Frontier 146
  11.2 Embracing the Human Element 149
        11.2.1 A Human-Centric Approach to Encryption 149
        11.2.2 Empowering Individuals in Digital Security 150
        11.2.3 Privacy by Design: A Step Towards
                Reconciliation 150
        11.2.4 Implementing Privacy by Design Involves 150
        11.2.5 Empowering Individual Privacy and Autonomy 151
        11.2.6 Resisting Surveillance Overreach 151
        11.2.7 Promoting Digital Literacy and Inclusivity 151
        11.2.8 Responsible Innovation and Collaboration 152
        11.2.9 A Moral Compass for Technology Companies 152
  11.3 A Harmonious Synthesis 152

11.3.1 *Embracing the Shadows 153*

11.3.2 *A Balanced Vision: Coexisting with Cryptography 153*

11.3.3 *The Path towards a Human-Centered Cryptography 154*

11.3.4 *Securing the Future While Respecting the Essence of Humanity 154*

12 Technical Notes   **155**

12.1 *Cryptography and Its Types 155*

    12.1.1 *Symmetric Key Cryptography 155*

    12.1.2 *Asymmetric Key Cryptography (Public-Key Cryptography) 156*

    12.1.3 *Hash Functions 156*

    12.1.4 *Message Authentication Codes (MACs) 156*

    12.1.5 *Digital Signatures 157*

12.2 *Uses of Cryptography 157*

12.3 *User Authentication Process 159*

12.4 *Hacking a User Account 160*

12.5 *User Account Compromises 161*

12.6 *Cryptography and Authentication 163*

12.7 *Cryptography and CRA 164*

    12.7.1 *Setup 164*

    12.7.2 *Challenge Phase 164*

    12.7.3 *Response Phase 165*

    12.7.4 *Initialization 166*

    12.7.5 *User Registration 166*

    12.7.6 *The Challenge–Response Process 166*

    12.7.7 *Response Calculation 166*

    12.7.8 *Response Submission and Verification 167*

    12.7.9 *Key Points 167*

12.8 *Hacking CRA 167*

    12.8.1 *Python Code for HMAC Real-World Implementation of Challenge–Response Authentication 169*

12.9 *Clarifications on ManusCrypt 174*

Appendix   177

List of Figures & Tables   177

Bibliography   179

Index   185

Foreword

There is no doubt that information technology has brought about a revolution around the world within the last few decades. As with the first industrial revolution, we have always tried to scurry ourselves into the future with the succeeding revolutions. Everyone knows that we are amidst the fourth industrial revolution and as usual are hurrying into the future, as if by sheer habit rather than by careful consideration.

It is against this backdrop that the author has presented a new perspective on the state of affairs of the information security arena. He takes us on a journey into cryptography right from its inception till the latest developments to date. With this he draws our attention to the poignant fact staring at our faces—*if ancient ciphers were originally designed by and for the humans, then why is modern cryptography not?* He puts forward this glaring design flaw replete with practical examples and use cases.

The best part is that he doesn't stop here but goes on to provide a very pragmatic solution via "anthropocentric information security". It is a first of its kind thought process that has never been discussed so openly and directly. Game theory, Nash equilibrium, hypergame theory, human factors engineering, human–machine interaction, man–machine interface—all of these fail to address the basic question at hand. *Why must we change our behavior in accordance to the machines that we have ourselves designed? Isn't that counterintuitive?* If these types of burning questions raise an intrigue in you then go ahead to the next chapter, else please place it back on the shelf as this is not made for you.

The book contains technical concepts at a high level with a simple and lucid presentation so that it is suited for both the layman as well as practitioners of information technology. Moreover, this is a book about possibilities and more than anything it is about putting the human back at the center of the industrial revolution.

Dr. Satasurya
Chairman, NSL

Preface

We are currently in the midst of the fourth industrial revolution. You probably would have heard of terms like "IR 4.0", "Web 3.0", "emerging technologies", etc. Never in the history of mankind have we witnessed such a fast-paced change in the landscape of human evolution. Yes, this is about human evolution and not just the information technology revolution.

Mankind is literally at a crossroads today, where civilization and technology are meeting head on. One wrong turn and we will be doomed forever. No, this is not a prophecy but a careful analysis of the big picture about the future ahead of us all. *As the global village leaps ahead to the dawn of a new world order, we are at a greater risk of losing out in the rat race between consumerism, profiteering, and interconnectedness as one race.*

Let me clarify that this book is not a sermon on ethics and morality in the age of unprecedented revolution powered by technology. Since there is so much hype about the fourth industrial revolution that is geared towards ushering in a "technological singularity", which will eventually lead to "transhumanism", it is very important to have another look at our journey so far. This book is all about putting the human being back at the center of this revolution. For this very purpose, a conceptual framework of "anthropocentric information security" has been presented.

Now, what is meant by "anthropocentric information security"? Does it mean that our systems must be so simple that an average person must be able to understand everything in the processes that drives it? That's an absolute NO. Let me clarify that when you type on your keyboard, what you are actually doing is just toggling with voltages. It is the underlying process that translates those specific voltages into ones and zeroes that then go into assembly language at the hardware level and further into programming languages at the OS and application level, which finally gets translated into the user interface, which generates the final output that is understandable by the user. So, we as average users are not supposed to oversee or even understand the entire process. Even as a software developer, one is only concerned with the given frame of reference and is not required to understand the hardware processes beneath his coding practice. Hence, here we are not toying around with the existing complex processes and systems involved, but in fact trying to redesign the system in its entirety, which is focused towards increasing the comfort and ease of the end user and at the same time minimizing the possible risks of any sort of compromise that can occur with the operations.

There will be many who will meet with cognitive dissonance after reading the contents of this book as it may not coincide with the popular narratives and their understanding of cryptography as it is. Only the captain of the ship knows how hard it is to moor the ship in the opposite direction at short notice, in the face of an imminent danger. Likewise, my concept of "ManusCrypt" will be hard to digest for those who are habituated (read: expert IT practitioners) to old ways (read: standard or universal methods or processes or protocols) and are unable to see the clear and present danger (read: "technological apocalypse") ahead of all of us. Thus, it is imperative that one has to grasp the concept presented herein with an open mind that welcomes fresh ideas. The reader is advised to be as skeptical as the author is as open to criticism and scrutiny. Let me also mention this—be it a product, process or even a person for that matter, an opinion from an unfamiliar outsider always brings benefits by exposing the routinely unseen or ignored faults. Audits, inspections and reviews are based on this very fact and are encouraged across the spectrum of every industry on the planet. In a similar manner, though not belonging to the cybersecurity fraternity directly, I have had the opportunity to perform information security audits (second and third party) for quite a few of my clients in my career. This has enabled me to look at this practice / arena with a bird's-eye view or from a neutral perspective. It is this very reason that I'm able to see clearly what even experts might be missing in their usual setup.

Here's a quote from one of the greatest thinkers of the century to dissuade you from buying or reading this book:

Whoever writes for fools, always finds a large public - Arthur Schopenhauer

Figure 0.1 Arthur Schopenhauer Quote.

To the rest, I am thankful to each one of you and welcome all types of criticism, discussion, and suggestions. Last but not least, even if some of you are able to empathize with "ManusCrypt" effectively, I will be grateful that my efforts are not in vain.

In order to give you a kick start, it is apt to quote Alan Turing here:

A computer would deserve to be called intelligent if it could deceive a human into believing that it was human
- Alan Turing

Figure 0.2 Alan Turing Quote 1.

Also, Alan Turing:

If a machine is expected to be infallible, it cannot also be intelligent
- Alan Turing

Figure 0.3 Alan Turing Quote 2.

From the previous two quotes by the "Father of AI", it is clear that *intelligence and fallibility must go hand in hand in order to facilitate biomimicry that is close to the human consciousness!*

Is the current IT paraphernalia even close to this? Let us find out together!

Dr. Prashant A U
Certified Management Consultant, Certified
Solutions Architect and Lead Auditor ISMS

Acknowledgments

I would like to express my sincere gratitude to the following individuals who played a significant role in bringing this book to fruition.

- **Dr. Satasuryaa:** My deepest thanks go to Dr. Satasuryaa, my mentor and guide throughout this journey. Your invaluable guidance, support, and encouragement have been instrumental in shaping this book. I am grateful for your patience, insightful feedback, and unwavering belief in my work.
- **Ms. Daisy Bala and Ms. Srividya Sethuraman:** I am indebted to Ms. Daisy Bala and Ms. Srividya Sethuraman for their willingness to review my manuscript. Your insightful comments and suggestions have helped me refine the content and ensure the book's clarity and coherence. I appreciate your time and expertise.
- **The Publishing Team:** My sincere thanks to the amazing publishing team—Ms. Gabriella, Ms. Radhika, and Ms. Aruna. Their professionalism, dedication, and meticulous attention to detail have been paramount in bringing this book to life. I am grateful for their expertise in editing, design, and marketing, and for their unwavering support throughout the publishing process.

The contributions from these individuals have been invaluable, and I am truly grateful for their support.

About the Author

Prashant A Upadhyaya is Postdoctoral Senior Research Fellow in Strategy at the National School of Leadership, Pune, India, and Fellow of the American Academy of Project Management, Colorado, USA. He is also an executive alumnus of IIM, Indore and IIT, Kanpur. He is a certified management consultant and a digital transformation advisor by profession. He is also a certified solutions architect, certified enterprise blockchain professional, certified API designer / security architect / product manager and lead auditor for information security management systems. He has 20 years of experience across several domains and has managed projects across Europe, Middle East, Africa, South Asia and Southeast Asia. He has been an auditor, consultant, and trainer for various MNCs, corporates, and SMEs. He has won two awards: "Bharat Ratna Dr. Radhakrishnan Gold Medal Award" from GEPRA, Chennai, India and "Best Researcher Award" from VPA, Chennai, India for his contribution to entrepreneurship and process improvement initiatives for SMEs, respectively. Apart from his profession, he is also a "Jyotish Vidya Vachaspati" and known to many as Pt. Vibhootinath.

In this book, he has tried to present a new paradigm where everything in the arena of information technology is designed around humans. He has also authored two other books: *Ternicode: Law of Three* (genre: leadership / business management) and *Swarbhanu Rahasya: Role of Nodes in Destiny* (genre: Astrology / Indology).

Introduction

0.0 MISE-EN-SCÈNE

Just like Tulsidas existed during the times of Akbar or the fact that Tesla, Edison and Swami Vivekananda were contemporaries or during the Mongol invasions of west Asia and Europe, there were several powerful dynasties in India like the Hoysalas, Chalukyas, Pandyas, Kakatiyas, Chandelas, Rashtrakutas, and several others; a complete picture of the times and events or a 360 degree view is seldom provided in history textbooks for reasons unknown; a similar approach is pursued in the business world in the wake of consumerism, the public's attention is always narrowed down to the desired product rather than providing a larger overview of the available options.

This opening paragraph is an unlikely and unexpected one. This is definitely not a sermon on "consumerism". Let me clarify the term "consumerism":

- Trying to sell your product / service is not consumerism
- Aggressive marketing is not consumerism
- Even an attempt to push down the throat a mediocre product is not consumerism
- The ability to "manufacture consent" is "consumerism"
- The best form of consumerism is when there is "manufactured consent" without your (i.e., the average consumer) awareness

Since a consumerist society and world is still in the grip of consumerism, it becomes imperative to remove the veil before getting a fresh breath of air. Moreover, information technology is no exception. Although IT has been an enabler and one of the major drivers of rapid change, it has been growing within the consumerist framework that we live in. Hence, sometimes one needs to begin with an out-of-context narrative in order to set the context with the proper perspective. So, let's continue in the same manner.

DOI: 10.1201/9781003527220-1

1

History textbooks and the business world have their respective limitations when it comes to providing a comprehensive and unbiased view of events or products. Let us explore the parallels between the two domains and delve into the reasons behind their narrow focus. *It is argued that a 360-degree perspective is essential in both contexts to foster critical thinking, promote a deeper understanding of the subject matter, and enable individuals to make informed decisions.*

0.1 HISTORICAL TEXTBOOKS' LIMITATIONS

a. **Selective Narratives:** History textbooks often present a curated version of events, influenced by cultural, political, or ideological biases. This selective narrative can downplay or even omit crucial historical events and figures, thereby limiting students' understanding of the full historical context.

b. **Eurocentrism:** Many history textbooks tend to focus predominantly on Western history, relegating the histories of other civilizations and cultures to the background. This Eurocentric approach deprives students of a broader view of the world's diverse historical experiences.

c. **Simplified Complexities:** History textbooks may simplify complex historical events, leading to an oversimplified and one-dimensional understanding. As a result, students might not grasp the intricate sociopolitical dynamics that shaped historical periods.

d. **Overemphasis on Empires and Monarchs:** The focus on prominent empires and monarchs often overshadows the contributions and struggles of ordinary people, women, and marginalized communities, leading to an incomplete understanding of history.

In a similar manner, the industrial revolution including the digital revolution has been governed and funneled through the lens of consumerism. No breakthrough ever has occurred without the will of the giants in Silicon Valley, without the attention of the elitist schools, without the consent of the developed nations, and without the patronage of those in power.

0.2 BUSINESS CONSUMERISM'S LIMITATIONS

a. **Manipulative Marketing:** In the business world, companies often employ manipulative marketing strategies to direct consumers' attention toward specific products or services. These strategies can create artificial demand and foster consumerism while ignoring alternative options.

b. **Product-Centric Approach:** Businesses may prioritize promoting their flagship products or services, limiting consumer exposure to alternative or more suitable options that might better meet their needs.

c. **Influencer Culture:** Influencer marketing often amplifies certain products, influencing consumers' perceptions and choices, while leaving lesser-known or innovative alternatives in the shadows.

d. **Short-Term Focus:** Many businesses are driven by short-term profit motives, leading to a focus on products with immediate returns rather than long-term sustainable solutions that might not gain immediate popularity.

0.3 IMPORTANCE OF A 360-DEGREE VIEW

a. **Critical Thinking and Informed Decision-Making:** Encouraging a 360-degree view in history education and consumerism empowers individuals to think critically, question prevailing narratives, and make informed decisions based on a deeper understanding of the subject matter.

b. **Appreciation of Diverse Perspectives:** Emphasizing a broader view of history and product options allows individuals to appreciate the richness of diverse cultures, contributions, and possibilities.

c. **Fostering Innovation:** In both history and business, a comprehensive understanding of the past or the range of products available can inspire innovation and creativity by drawing on a broader pool of knowledge and experiences.

d. **Holistic Understanding:** A 360-degree view promotes a holistic understanding of complex historical processes and product landscapes, enabling individuals to grasp the interconnectedness of various elements and systems.

The limited scope of history textbooks and consumerist marketing strategies can hinder individuals' ability to form well-rounded perspectives. Emphasizing a 360-degree view in history education and business consumerism is crucial for nurturing critical thinking, appreciating diverse perspectives, fostering innovation, and gaining a holistic understanding of the world. As consumers and learners, we must actively seek out diverse sources of information to enrich our knowledge and make well-informed decisions based on a comprehensive understanding of the available options.

0.4 PERSPECTIVES, CHANGE MANAGEMENT, AND PARADIGM SHIFT

0.4.1 Perspectives and Historical Context

A 360-degree view in history education encourages students to consider multiple perspectives and examine events within their historical context. By understanding the diverse viewpoints of different actors and societies, students gain a more nuanced understanding of historical events. This approach fosters empathy and helps avoid a judgmental attitude based on contemporary values. Moreover, it enables students to appreciate the complexities and contradictions inherent in historical processes, acknowledging that history is not a straightforward narrative but a tapestry of interconnected stories.

Similarly, in the business world, considering multiple perspectives is crucial for effective change management. When organizations undergo change, they impact employees, stakeholders, and customers. A myopic view of change can lead to resistance and misunderstandings, hindering the success of initiatives. By adopting a 360-degree perspective, businesses can anticipate and address concerns, ensure transparency, and engage stakeholders collaboratively, leading to smoother change management.

0.4.2 Change Management and Historical Transformations

Change management is not just relevant in the business world; it is also a fundamental aspect of historical transformations. Societies have undergone radical changes over time, such as revolutions, industrialization, and globalization. Understanding how these historical shifts unfolded and their lasting impacts is crucial for navigating present-day challenges.

History also teaches us that paradigms shift over time. Societal norms, values, and beliefs evolve, and what was once accepted as the norm may undergo radical changes. A 360-degree view of history allows us to witness paradigm shifts and understand the factors that contributed to their occurrence. This historical perspective can be valuable in the business world, where industries and markets are subject to constant transformation. Businesses that can anticipate and adapt to paradigm shifts are more likely to thrive in an ever-changing landscape.

0.4.3 Paradigm Shift in Consumerism

The business world has experienced significant paradigm shifts in consumerism. Traditional marketing and advertising have given way to digital marketing, influencer culture, and e-commerce. The rise of conscious consumerism has also led to a growing demand for sustainable and ethically produced products. A 360-degree view of consumerism enables businesses to identify these shifts and respond proactively to changing consumer preferences.

In a historical context, paradigm shifts have often been driven by major technological advancements, social movements, and changes in governance. These shifts have reshaped societies, economies, and cultures. By studying history with a 360-degree approach, we can recognize patterns and potential trajectories that can inform decision-making in the business world.

Perspectives, change management, and paradigm shifts are interconnected concepts that bridge the gap between history and the business world. Emphasizing a 360-degree view in both domains encourages critical thinking, promotes empathy, and enables a deeper understanding of the complexities involved. By learning from historical transformations and considering diverse perspectives, businesses can navigate change effectively and adapt to paradigm shifts in consumerism. Likewise, a holistic understanding of history equips individuals with the knowledge and insight to make informed decisions and contribute positively to the ever-changing world around them.

Now, the obvious question is this—how are consumerism, perspectives, manipulation, etc., related to information technology strategy viz. information security? Is there really a need to focus on "anthropocentric information security"? Aren't the modern machines of today complementing and assisting the humans? Haven't we progressed so far as to have reached a crossroads where technology is in a position to challenge humanity at large?

If you are intrigued by these questions, then read on to understand the reality as it is presented with the veil of ignorance and brouhaha removed from the subject matter.

0.5 CURRENT STATE OF AFFAIRS

Now that the context is set, we can come back to our main topic. Anthropocentric information technology has been limited to the following as of now:

0.5.1 Human–Machine Interaction (HMI) in Information Technology

Human–machine interaction, also known as human–computer interaction (HCI) or human–computer interaction design (HCID), is a multidisciplinary field within information technology that focuses on the design, evaluation, and improvement of computer systems and technology interfaces to enhance the interaction between humans and machines. The primary goal of HMI is to create user-friendly, efficient, and effective interfaces that allow users to interact with technology in a natural and intuitive manner.

Key aspects of human–machine interaction in the context of information technology include:

User Interface (UI) Design: Designing the graphical and interactive elements of software applications, websites, and other digital platforms to ensure they are visually appealing, easy to navigate, and promote a positive user experience.

User Experience (UX) Design: Considering the overall experience of users while interacting with technology, including their emotions, perceptions, and satisfaction, with the aim of optimizing usability and user satisfaction.

Interaction Techniques: Exploring different ways users can interact with machines, such as through touch interfaces, voice commands, gestures, or virtual reality.

Accessibility: Ensuring that technology interfaces are accessible to all users, including those with disabilities, by implementing features like screen readers, keyboard navigation, and adjustable font sizes.

Feedback Mechanisms: Providing timely and relevant feedback to users to inform them about the system's status and actions, helping them understand how their interactions affect the technology.

User-Centered Design: Involving users throughout the design process to understand their needs, preferences, and pain points, and incorporating this knowledge into the development of the technology.

0.5.2 Human Factors Engineering in Information Technology

Human factors engineering (HFE), also known as ergonomics, is a scientific discipline that examines the interaction between humans and technology, products, or systems. In the context of information technology, HFE focuses on optimizing the design of computer systems and software to ensure they are well suited to human capabilities and limitations. The objective is to enhance user performance, safety, and comfort while using technology.

Key aspects of human factors engineering in the context of information technology include:

Task Analysis: Understanding the tasks users need to perform with technology and designing systems that support efficient and error-free task completion.

Cognitive Workload: Assessing the mental demands placed on users by the technology and reducing cognitive load to prevent information overload and cognitive fatigue.

Error Prevention and Recovery: Implementing design features that prevent user errors and allow for easy recovery if errors occur.

Physical Ergonomics: Considering the physical comfort and well-being of users while interacting with computer hardware, such as ergonomic keyboard and mouse design.

Display Design: Optimizing the layout, size, and contrast of visual displays to minimize eye strain and enhance readability.

Usability Testing: Conducting usability studies and user testing to identify design flaws and gather feedback for improvement.

Both human–machine interaction and human factors engineering play crucial roles in the development of information technology, helping to create technology that is user friendly, efficient, and enhances the overall user experience. By considering human capabilities and limitations, IT professionals can design systems that effectively meet the needs of users and align with their behaviors and preferences.

However, HFE, HMI, and similar other concepts serve only as just another feature rather than being at the core of design. This book is a small attempt to change exactly that.

0.6 WHY SHOULD YOU READ THIS BOOK?

While modern technologies like AI, ML, ChatGPT, LLM, and deepfakes offer numerous benefits, there are valid concerns about the ways in which users are asked to adapt to these technologies instead of the other way around. Here are some reasons why these technologies may be considered futile in that sense:

0.6.1 Complexity and Learning Curve

Many of these technologies require users to have a certain level of technical knowledge and skills to interact effectively. For instance, users are asked to learn "prompt engineering" to engage with AI chatbots, which can be a barrier for nontechnical individuals.

0.6.2 Lack of Intuitive Interfaces

The interfaces of some technologies may not be user friendly or intuitive. Users often find themselves having to understand complex processes or use specific commands to achieve their desired outcomes, making the overall user experience less accessible.

0.6.3 Limited Customization

Users often have limited control over the customization of these technologies. Instead of adapting to individual user preferences and needs, users may find themselves constrained by predefined algorithms and models that may not align with their unique requirements.

0.6.4 Bias and Fairness Concerns

Many AI and ML systems inherit biases present in their training data, potentially leading to biased outcomes. Users may find themselves facing discriminatory or unfair results, highlighting the need for these technologies to be more adaptive to diverse user backgrounds and perspectives.

0.6.5 Ethical Challenges

Deepfakes and similar technologies pose ethical challenges, as they can be used to manipulate and deceive. Users may feel compelled to adapt to a world where discerning between real and fake content becomes increasingly difficult, rather than having technologies designed to prevent or mitigate such issues.

0.6.6 Invasion of Privacy

Some technologies, such as facial recognition powered by AI, may lead to concerns about privacy invasion. Users may be asked to adapt to a world where their every move is monitored rather than having technologies that prioritize privacy by design.

0.6.7 Job Displacement

The integration of AI and automation technologies in the workforce may lead to job displacement for certain professions. Users may be required to adapt to new roles or acquire new skills, potentially leaving some individuals behind in the process.

0.6.8 Inflexibility in Problem-Solving

While AI and ML can excel in specific tasks, they may lack the flexibility and creativity that humans possess in problem-solving. Users may find themselves adapting to a more rigid problem-solving approach rather than benefiting from the complementary strengths of human intelligence and machine capabilities.

0.6.9 Overreliance on Technology

There's a risk of overreliance on these technologies, with users potentially becoming overly dependent on AI and ML systems. This dependence may hinder critical thinking and decision-making skills, as users adapt to a mindset of relying on technology for answers.

0.6.10 Disconnect from Human Interaction

As chatbots and language models become more prevalent, there's a concern about a potential decline in meaningful human-to-human interactions. Users might adapt to a world where human connection is mediated by technology, potentially leading to social and emotional disconnection.

In summary, there are valid concerns about the impact of these technologies on user adaptation rather than accommodating human needs and preferences. Balancing technological advancements with user-centric design and ethical considerations is crucial for ensuring a positive and inclusive future with these technologies.

The tenth point focuses on the concern that modern technologies, particularly AI chatbots and language models, may contribute to a disconnect from meaningful human interaction. Here's a detailed explanation with examples:

0.7 DISCONNECT FROM HUMAN INTERACTION

0.7.1 Description

As AI chatbots and language models become more prevalent, there is a growing concern that users may adapt to a world where human interaction is increasingly mediated by technology. This could lead to a decline in authentic, emotionally rich connections between individuals.

0.7.2 Examples

0.7.2.1 Automated Customer Support

Many companies are implementing AI-driven chatbots for customer support. While these chatbots can provide quick responses, they often lack the empathy and nuanced understanding that a human customer service representative can offer. Users adapting to this technology may experience frustration or dissatisfaction in situations where a personal touch is needed.

0.7.2.2 Social Media Interactions

AI algorithms on social media platforms curate content based on user preferences. This can create echo chambers, where users are exposed to information and opinions that align with their existing views. Instead of diverse human interactions, users may adapt to a digital environment that reinforces their existing beliefs, limiting exposure to different perspectives.

0.7.2.3 Online Dating Apps

Dating apps often use algorithms to match users based on their preferences and behavior. While these algorithms aim to improve compatibility, they may oversimplify the complexities of human relationships. Users adapting to these technologies may find that the initial matching process doesn't always translate into meaningful and lasting connections.

0.7.2.4 Virtual Assistants and Companions

With the rise of AI-powered virtual assistants and companions, users might adapt to relying on technology for emotional support. While these systems can simulate conversation, they lack genuine emotions and understanding. Users may find themselves adapting to a world where the comfort of human interaction is replaced by simulated responses.

0.7.2.5 Educational Chatbots

In the realm of education, chatbots are being used to assist students with learning. While they can provide information and answer questions, they may lack the interpersonal skills and encouragement that a human teacher or mentor can offer. Users adapting to educational chatbots might miss out on the motivational and supportive aspects of human guidance.

0.7.2.6 Professional Networking Platforms

AI-driven algorithms on professional networking platforms recommend connections based on users' profiles and activities. While this can facilitate networking, users might adapt to a system where connections are driven by algorithms rather than organic, human-driven relationships, potentially diluting the authenticity of professional networks.

0.7.2.7 Emotion Recognition Technology

Some technologies claim to recognize and respond to users' emotions, such as sentiment analysis in text or facial recognition for emotional cues. While these tools aim to enhance user experience, they may oversimplify complex human emotions, leading to misinterpretations and a lack of genuine emotional understanding.

0.7.3 Concerns

- **Emotional Depth:** Users may adapt to interactions that lack the emotional depth and understanding that humans naturally bring to conversations.
- **Loss of Genuine Connection:** Over time, users may find themselves adapting to a digital landscape where genuine, unmediated human connections become rarer.
- **Impact on Social Skills:** There is a risk that reliance on AI-driven interactions might impact users' social skills, as face-to-face communication and emotional intelligence are essential for healthy human relationships.

In addressing this concern, it is crucial for developers and designers to prioritize technologies that enhance, rather than replace, human connections.

Striking a balance between efficiency and the emotional richness of human interaction will be vital for creating a positive and sustainable future with these technologies.

This book is all about keeping humans at the center, rather than asking humans to adapt to newer technologies. So, if this is of concern to you, please go ahead and enjoy the journey presented in this book.

0.8 THE MECHANICAL TURK

It was the 18th century and inventions were galore with giant leaps in scientific temper leading to an era of industrialization for the next century. A time when stuff like the diesel engine, stethoscope, telephone, Portland cement, battery and many other useful things were being invented, there existed an "Automaton Chess Player" also known as "the Mechanical Turk".

The invention was designed by Hungarian engineer and inventor Baron Wolfgang von Kempelen in 1769. The machine was introduced as a chess-playing automaton capable of beating even the strongest challengers. In response to a challenge, Wolfgang was keen to impress Maria Theresa, the empress of Austria–Hungary and, hence, had vowed to build the apparatus whose magic would surpass every other thing seen before.

Figure 0.4 Mechanical Turk Front View.

The automaton first made its appearance in 1770 at the Habsburg Court in Vienna, where it beat all comers in chess at that exhibition. This act would be repeated countess times across Europe and the US for the next 84 years even as it changed hands from Kempelen to a Bavarian showman, Johann Maelzel. Maelzel later took the automaton to the US in 1826, where the saga continued until it reached a Chinese museum in Philadelphia where it was burnt by fire in 1854.

It was a four-foot cabinet with a life-sized wooden figure dressed in Ottoman attire holding a smoking pipe in the left hand, with the right hand resting on the table. The cabinet's interior was crammed with a series of gears, cranks, and levers that resembled the innards of a clock. It was a mechanical robot capable of reasoning and playing one of the world's most intellectual board games, i.e., chess. It had displayed ingenious capabilities and had achieved the impossible fame of defeating most of its opponents in the game of chess. While it had several critics who claimed that all its moves were orchestrated by a hidden human operator, nothing or no one could stop its success at exhibitions, shows, and large gatherings.

Amongst the notable opponents it had defeated were eminent personalities like Napolean Bonaparte, Russian czar Paul I, and Benjamin Franklin.

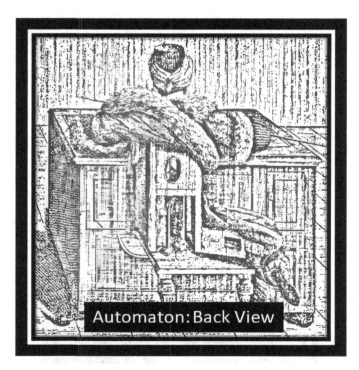

Figure 0.5 Mechanical Turk Back View.

Amongst the witnesses too were celebrities like Joseph II, Edgar Allan Poe, and Ludwig van Beethoven.

It was later on accepted that the critics were indeed right and amongst its operators were chess masters like Johann Allgaier, Boncourt, Aaron Alexandre, William Lewis, Jacques Mouret, and William Schlumberger.

However, the operators within the mechanism during Wolfgang von Kempelen's original tour remain a mystery. The secret of this hoax was that a normal-sized man could recline and hide within the machine and remain unseen by the audience by repositioning himself using a sliding seat. Later on, the operator would return to the chamber, light a candle, follow the progress of the game outside by watching a series of dangling metal discs being attracted to magnets in the base of the chess pieces and would make moves by a series of levers that could move the Turk's arm and open and close its fingers.

The Turkman's story is a glaring example of the unwittingly brilliant use of HMI (human–machine interaction) and gest for enacting a make-believe reality. Without the gest, the machine would have met with utter failure in spite of the ingenious mechanism involved in its operation. The main objective of starting with this story about a hoax is to set a conducive

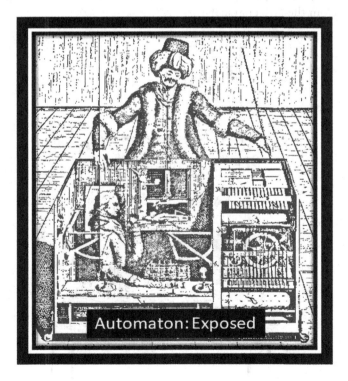

Figure 0.6 Mechanical Turk Exposed View.

environment that will enable the readers to open up to a new perspective for understanding the forthcoming concept.

Let's try to see the hoax the way it was designed—designed for the machine! The false narratives that were peddled, before the machine could display its claimed capabilities, were designed to fool the audience in every possible manner. The support and sponsorship of authorities, traditional parlor tricks, gimmickry, showmanship, advertising, and every other possible illusion were employed to convince the general public of its assurance of performance and absolute awe. What is, unfortunately, more interesting is that this kind of quirky business dragged on for over eight decades. There are some protagonists who argue that the automaton was an inspiration and a precursor to computers and that it bridged the gap between fact and fiction that was necessary to bring about "required" change. However, in my opinion a hoax can never be an inspiration for anything worthwhile and can only be a bridge to downfall.

In stark contrast, from the Torres' Chess Machine in 1912 to Turing's Turbochamp in 1950 to IBM's DeepBlue in 1996, we have come a long way in the process of "Biomimicry". From the early computers to the modern-day AI, we are still working with APUs, i.e., algorithmic processing units. Hence, at a very fundamental level everything that we have built so far is not much different from the "Mechanical Turk".

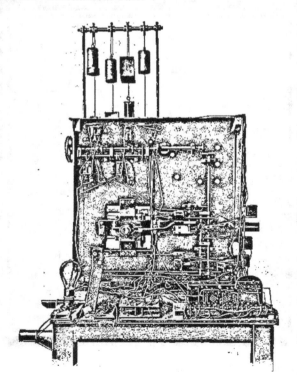

Figure 0.7 Torres' Chess Machine.

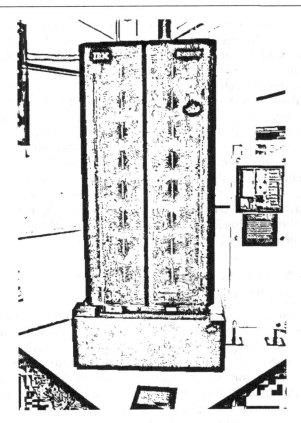

Figure 0.8 IBM DeepBlue.

I do know that several eyebrows will be raised upon my previous statement. In the age of AlphaGo–DeepMind, it will seem preposterous to even raise a question mark to the recent developments in the realm of information technology. You will need to have some patience and an open mind to be able to absorb the contents presented further in this book.

0.9 SETTING THE STAGE

Moving on from the story to the central subject, information security is all about encryption and encryption is all based on cryptography. Let us analyze the role of cryptography and its relation vis-à-vis humans.

0.9.1 The Ubiquitous Presence of Cryptography

In the vast landscape of the digital age, cryptography has emerged as an omnipresent force, woven into the very fabric of our interconnected world. From securing online transactions and protecting sensitive data to ensuring the confidentiality of our communications, modern cryptography has become an indispensable tool in our daily lives. However, amidst the allure of enhanced security and convenience, there exists a growing concern about the impact of cryptography on our humanity.

In today's interconnected world, cryptography has become an inseparable part of our daily lives. From the moment we send a text message, make an online purchase, or log into a social media platform, cryptography silently weaves a web of protection around our digital interactions.

Cryptography, derived from the Greek words "kryptós" (hidden) and "gráphein" (to write), is the science and art of securing information through the use of mathematical algorithms. Its origins can be traced back to ancient civilizations, where secret codes were employed to safeguard critical messages from adversaries. Over the centuries, cryptography has evolved from simple substitution ciphers to complex algorithms that defy decryption without the proper keys.

0.9.2 The Balance between Security and Human Privacy

As we delve into the realm of modern cryptography, we encounter a delicate balance between security and human privacy. The quest for unbreakable codes and robust encryption mechanisms has led to a paradigm shift in how we perceive and protect information. Yet, at what cost does this pursuit come? The more we fortify our digital fortresses, the more we may unintentionally isolate ourselves from the very essence of human connection.

The ubiquity of cryptography in the digital age presents a delicate balance between security imperatives and human privacy. On one hand, robust encryption technologies offer protection against cyber threats, safeguarding sensitive data from unauthorized access and malicious actors. Financial transactions, healthcare records, and confidential communications are shielded from prying eyes, fostering trust in digital interactions.

On the other hand, the growing importance of cryptography in securing modern systems has sparked debates surrounding privacy and civil liberties. Governments and corporations seek to protect their citizens and customers from cyberattacks, terrorism, and organized crime. However, the demand for exceptional access to encrypted data by law enforcement agencies has raised concerns about potential surveillance overreach and the erosion of individual privacy rights.

0.9.3 The Duality of Modern Cryptography

Modern cryptography embodies a duality that cannot be ignored. On one hand, it empowers individuals and organizations with the means to safeguard their sensitive data from prying eyes, ensuring confidentiality and integrity. It is the bedrock of secure communication, enabling freedom of expression and protecting dissidents and whistleblowers who dare to challenge the status quo.

On the other hand, as we delve deeper into the digital realm, we expose ourselves to a complex web of surveillance, data breaches, and erosion of personal privacy. Encryption, designed to provide safety and confidentiality, can also become a double-edged sword, used to conceal nefarious activities and hinder legitimate investigations.

In this book, we embark on a journey to unveil the often overlooked aspects of modern cryptography—the ways in which it challenges our very humanity. We will explore how the exponential growth of technology has amplified the impact of cryptography on human society, for better and for worse.

From individuals to nations, cryptography influences the power dynamics that shape our world. It fuels debates on the ethical implications of surveillance and raises questions about the delicate balance between individual rights and national security. As governments and corporations vie for control over vast troves of digital information, we are confronted with the ethical dilemmas of striking the right chord between privacy and the greater good.

Modern cryptography embodies a duality that reflects its dual impact on society. While encryption technologies empower individuals with secure communications and privacy, they also pose challenges for law enforcement in investigating criminal activities. The balance between individual rights and public safety has become a central point of contention, igniting discussions among policymakers, technologists, and civil society.

Cryptographers continually strive to develop stronger encryption algorithms to protect against potential threats, while governments grapple with the need for responsible regulation that respects individual rights and fosters a safe digital environment.

0.9.4 The Transformation of Communication

With the advent of digital communication, the way we interact with each other has undergone a seismic shift. Messages once written on parchment and sealed with wax have been replaced by instant messaging and encrypted emails. The privacy of our thoughts and opinions is now enshrined within the digital vaults of cryptographic algorithms.

But, as we embrace the convenience of digital communication, have we also unknowingly sacrificed the richness of human connection? How does modern cryptography impact the authenticity and vulnerability that underpins our relationships? Is our relentless pursuit of convenience eclipsing the value of personal communication and face-to-face interactions?

0.9.5 The Human Equation in Encryption

The human element in the realm of encryption is both a strength and a vulnerability. Human errors in managing cryptographic keys and practices can lead to catastrophic data breaches. Moreover, our instinctive need for trust, transparency, and social interaction often clashes with the faceless algorithms that govern our digital lives.

Throughout this journey, we will explore the psychological implications of living in a world governed by cryptography. The constant awareness of surveillance and the fear of cyberattacks have given rise to a phenomenon known as "cybersecurity anxiety". Understanding these emotional undercurrents is essential as we seek a harmonious coexistence between technology and humanity.

In the following chapters, we will examine the ethical, social, and political dimensions of cryptography. We will ponder the consequences of living in a world where every message is encrypted, and privacy is both a fundamental right and an ever-debatable concept.

Together, let us venture into the depths of modern cryptography and unravel the shadows it casts upon humanity. In doing so, we may uncover new insights that can help us find the path toward a world where technology and human values coalesce harmoniously.

As we embark on a journey into the realm of cryptography, we must recognize its pervasive presence in our lives and the intricate ethical questions it poses. Striking a balance between security and human privacy is a dynamic challenge that requires thoughtful consideration and collaboration from all stakeholders.

Throughout this exploration, we will delve into the history, challenges, and ethical dimensions of modern cryptography. From the ancient secrets of Caesar ciphers to the cutting-edge algorithms of today, cryptography continues to shape our interactions and perceptions of privacy in an increasingly interconnected world. Let us now journey further into the intricate web of cryptography, seeking to understand its profound impact on humanity and the path towards a harmonious digital future.

0.10 EPISTLE FOR BIBLIOPHILES

Before we proceed further, it is very important to pause and mention here that this book has been written in a largely unstructured manner. The reason being the following:

- It is about changing perspectives
- It is about a paradigm shift
- It is not about what is or what will be

- It is about restructuring the very roots of the subject matter
- It is not a reference material for the subject matter
- It is a proposal quite divergent from the general views
- It is about knowledge and not about conditioning
- It does not claim to educate the reader, rather it is aimed at raising awareness
- As opposed to formal education, schooling, or even professional training, it is about sparking that inquisitiveness in you that has been lying dormant after years of indoctrination

Hence, I would love to be excused for not conforming to what most readers are accustomed to given the times and tidings.

This quote from Richard P. Feynmann seems apt here:

Study hard what interests you the most in the most undisciplined, irreverent and original manner possible
- Richard P Feynman

Figure 0.9 Richard Feynman Quote.

Chapter 1

Need for Secrecy
and Its History

1.1 WHY SECRECY?

> "The secret to success is to not to let anyone else in on the secret."
> —Anonymous

Anyone desirous of success is well aware of the importance of secrecy. You always make hay while the sun shines rather than going around declaring that you are going to make hay while the sun is shining.

Secrecy, the act of intentionally withholding or concealing information, has been a pervasive aspect of human societies throughout history. Its origins can be traced back to various factors, including the need for survival, security, power dynamics, and the preservation of sensitive knowledge or technologies. Here's a brief overview of the need for secrecy and its origins:

    1.1.1. Survival and Security: In the early stages of human development, secrecy played a crucial role in ensuring the survival of individuals

Figure 1.1 Secret.

DOI: 10.1201/9781003527220-2

and groups. Concealing important information, such as the location of food sources or shelter, helped protect against potential threats from rivals or predators. As societies evolved, secrecy became instrumental in safeguarding military strategies, intelligence, and state secrets to maintain national security.

1.1.2. **Power and Control:** Secrecy has long been associated with power and control. Rulers, leaders, and organizations often rely on secrecy to maintain their authority and suppress opposition. Hidden knowledge can grant an advantage in decision-making, negotiations, and the manipulation of public opinion. Secrecy has been used as a tool by governments, corporations, and influential individuals to protect their interests, maintain dominance, and thwart potential challengers.

1.1.3. **Trade Secrets and Intellectual Property:** Secrecy has played a crucial role in protecting trade secrets and intellectual property throughout history. Businesses and inventors have a vested interest in safeguarding proprietary information, formulas, manufacturing processes, and technological advancements. Secrecy ensures a competitive edge, encourages innovation, and allows organizations to profit from their unique creations.

1.1.4. **Espionage and Warfare:** The art of espionage, gathering intelligence through covert means, relies heavily on secrecy. Spies and intelligence agencies operate in the shadows, gathering classified information, infiltrating enemy organizations, and disrupting rival plans. Secrecy is also critical during times of war, enabling military forces to maintain the element of surprise, protect sensitive military operations, and confuse adversaries.

1.1.5. **Privacy and Personal Safety:** Secrecy is essential for safeguarding personal privacy and safety. Individuals may choose to keep personal information, such as financial details, health records, or private communications, confidential to prevent unauthorized access, identity theft, or potential harm. Secrecy also plays a role in protecting vulnerable populations, such as whistleblowers or individuals at risk of persecution or discrimination.

1.1.6. **Sacred and Occult Knowledge:** Secrecy has been associated with religious, mystical, and occult practices throughout history. Certain religious rituals, initiation ceremonies, and esoteric teachings are often kept secret to maintain their spiritual significance and exclusivity. Secrecy surrounding sacred texts or hidden knowledge within religious and spiritual traditions can foster a sense of mystery and reverence among believers.

It is important to note that while secrecy can serve legitimate purposes, it can also be misused, leading to corruption, manipulation, and violations of human rights. Balancing the need for secrecy with transparency and accountability remains an ongoing challenge for societies worldwide.

1.2 SECRECY IN COMMUNICATION

Any worthwhile enterprise cannot be executed without communication. All types of communication can be intercepted that can lead to the danger of exposing information to underserving parties. Hence, the secrecy element in communication is of utmost importance.

Throughout history, there have been numerous instances of secret communication methods and techniques employed to transmit confidential information. Here are a few notable historical examples:

1.2.1. **Caesar Cipher:** The Caesar cipher is one of the earliest known encryption techniques, attributed to Julius Caesar. It involves shifting each letter of the alphabet a certain number of positions to create a coded message. Caesar used this cipher to send military orders, ensuring that only those with the decryption key (the specific shift value) could understand the message.

1.2.2. **Atbash Cipher:** The Atbash cipher is a substitution cipher that replaces each letter of the alphabet with its mirror image. For instance, "A" becomes "Z", "B" becomes "Y", and so forth. It was used by ancient Hebrew scholars and is also found in other ancient cultures.

1.2.3. **Polybius Square:** Developed by the ancient Greek historian Polybius, the Polybius square is a substitution cipher that uses a grid with letters or symbols to encode messages. Each letter is represented by its coordinates in the grid. It was commonly used by the Greeks and Romans.

1.2.4. **Vigenère Cipher:** The Vigenère cipher is a polyalphabetic substitution cipher invented by the Italian scholar Giovan Battista Bellaso but popularized by Blaise de Vigenère, a French diplomat. It uses a keyword to determine different shift values for different positions in the message, making it more secure than simple substitution ciphers.

1.2.5. **Playfair Cipher:** Invented by Sir Charles Wheatstone but named after his friend Lord Playfair, the Playfair cipher is a digraph substitution cipher. It uses a 5 × 5 grid of letters, omitting "J", to encrypt pairs of letters in the message.

1.2.6. **Enigma Machine:** Developed in the early 20th century, the Enigma machine was a complex electromechanical device used by Nazi Germany during World War II to encrypt and decrypt secret messages. It employed a series of rotating wheels and electrical connections to scramble the letters of a message, making it extremely difficult for Allied cryptanalysts to decipher intercepted transmissions. The successful cracking of the Enigma code by British codebreakers at Bletchley Park played a significant role in the outcome of the war.

1.2.7. **Navajo Code Talkers:** During World War II, Navajo Native Americans played a crucial role in secure communication for the United States military. The Navajo language, with its complex syntax and few non-Navajo speakers, was used as a basis for an unbreakable code. Navajo Code Talkers transmitted sensitive information, such as troop movements and battle plans, using their native language, which proved highly effective in thwarting enemy interception and decryption efforts.

1.2.8. **One-Time Pads:** One-time pads are a form of encryption where a random key is used only once to encode and decode a message. This method was employed during the Cold War by intelligence agencies, such as the CIA and the KGB. The key, typically a sheet of random characters, would be shared securely between the sender and receiver, and each character would be combined with the corresponding character in the message to produce the encoded text. One-time pads are considered mathematically unbreakable when used correctly.

1.2.9. **Radio Free Europe:** During the Cold War, Radio Free Europe (RFE) served as a clandestine broadcasting service transmitting news, information, and propaganda to countries behind the Iron Curtain. RFE utilized various covert techniques to ensure its broadcasts reached the target audience without being jammed or intercepted by Soviet authorities. These methods included transmitting from aircraft or ships, using mobile broadcasting stations, and employing encryption and secure communication channels.

These examples demonstrate the ingenuity and importance of secret communication methods in various historical contexts, highlighting the lengths individuals and organizations have gone to protect sensitive information during times of conflict and espionage.

1.3 TYPES OF SECRECY IN MODERN COMMUNICATION

Secrecy in communication refers to the practice of concealing or encrypting information to prevent unauthorized access or interception by third parties. It is an essential aspect of maintaining privacy, protecting sensitive data, and ensuring secure communication channels. Here are a few key points about secrecy in communication:

Encryption: Encryption is the process of converting information into an unreadable format using cryptographic algorithms. Encrypted data can only be accessed and understood by authorized individuals who possess the decryption key. Encryption techniques are employed in various forms, such as secure messaging apps, virtual private networks

(VPNs), and secure email services, to protect the confidentiality of sensitive information.

Secure Communication Channels: Secrecy can be achieved by using secure communication channels that provide encryption and protection against eavesdropping. For example, Secure Sockets Layer (SSL) and Transport Layer Security (TLS) protocols are used to establish secure connections between web browsers and servers, ensuring that data transmitted during online transactions remains confidential.

Steganography: Steganography is the practice of hiding secret information within other non-secret data. This technique involves embedding messages or data within innocent-looking carriers, such as images, audio files, or even text documents. Steganography helps conceal the existence of hidden information, making it difficult for unauthorized individuals to detect or intercept the secret message.

Code Words and Ciphers: Throughout history, code words and ciphers have been employed to encode messages and ensure secrecy. These techniques involve substituting letters or words with symbols, numbers, or other characters according to predefined rules. Code words and ciphers can make the message unintelligible to anyone without the proper key or knowledge of the encryption method.

Secure Communication Networks: Secrecy in communication is facilitated by the use of secure networks. Virtual private networks (VPNs) create encrypted connections over public or untrusted networks, protecting the privacy of data transmitted between remote locations. Secure communication networks are crucial for businesses, governments, and individuals to ensure secure data transfer and remote access.

Confidentiality Agreements: In certain professional settings, confidentiality agreements or nondisclosure agreements (NDAs) are used to legally enforce secrecy. These agreements establish a contractual obligation for individuals or parties to protect and maintain the confidentiality of specific information or trade secrets.

While secrecy in communication is important for privacy and security, it is worth noting that in some cases, it can also raise ethical concerns. Governments and organizations must strike a balance between the need for secrecy and the importance of transparency, accountability, and protecting individual rights.

1.4 EVOLUTION OF MODERN CRYPTOGRAPHY

For starters, let us have a brief overview on the evolution of modern cryptography. We will discuss it in detail in the next chapter, which is bound to change your perception on the subject matter.

1.4.1 From Ancient Ciphers to RSA: A Historical Overview

To understand the complexities of modern cryptography, we must embark on a journey through time, tracing its evolution from the humble ancient ciphers to the groundbreaking algorithms of today. The roots of encryption stretch back to ancient civilizations, where secret messages and hidden communication were employed for military, diplomatic, and personal purposes.

In the annals of history, ancient ciphers were relatively simple and often relied on basic substitution or transposition techniques. The Caesar cipher, believed to be used by Julius Caesar himself, involved shifting each letter of the alphabet by a fixed number of positions to create an encrypted message. Similarly, the Skytale employed a transposition method by wrapping a long strip of parchment around a staff of a specific diameter to create an encrypted message.

As societies advanced, so did their cryptographic techniques. In the Middle Ages, Arab scholars made significant contributions to cryptography, developing methods for breaking ciphers and analyzing encrypted texts. The Renaissance brought innovations such as the Alberti Cipher Disk, which allowed for more efficient encryption and decryption processes.

The evolution of modern cryptography is a testament to human ingenuity and the relentless pursuit of secure communication. Building upon the foundations laid by ancient ciphers, cryptography has witnessed remarkable advancements over the centuries.

The Renaissance era marked a significant turning point, with polyalphabetic ciphers like the Vigenère cipher challenging cryptanalysts to develop new methods for breaking codes. In the 19th century, the invention of the electromechanical rotor-based Enigma machine by Arthur Scherbius demonstrated the power of encryption in military operations.

However, it was during the digital age that cryptography experienced revolutionary breakthroughs that transformed the field entirely.

1.4.2 The Digital Age: Pioneers and Revolutionary Breakthroughs

The advent of the digital age marked a turning point in the history of cryptography. With the invention of computers and the rise of electronic communication, traditional methods of encryption were rendered inadequate. It was during this time that modern cryptographic pioneers emerged, laying the foundation for the complex algorithms we rely on today.

In the mid-20th century, Claude Shannon, often regarded as the "father of modern cryptography", published groundbreaking works that established the mathematical foundations of cryptography. His work on information theory and communication introduced the concept of perfect secrecy, where the ciphertext provides no information about the plaintext without knowledge of the secret key.

The advent of computers in the mid-20th century propelled cryptography into a new era of possibilities. Pioneers such as Claude Shannon and Alan Turing laid the theoretical foundations for modern cryptography, exploring concepts like perfect secrecy and the limitations of computational power in breaking codes.

In the 1970s, the data encryption standard (DES) emerged as a landmark symmetric encryption algorithm, adopted by governments and businesses worldwide. Its substitution-permutation network design paved the way for secure data transmission and storage.

1.4.3 Public-Key Cryptography: The Pandora's Box of Data Privacy

One of the most significant breakthroughs in modern cryptography was the invention of public-key cryptography. In the 1970s, Whitfield Diffie and Martin Hellman proposed the concept of asymmetric key algorithms, where two distinct keys—one public and one private—are used for encryption and decryption. This revolutionary idea opened a Pandora's box of possibilities for secure communication.

The RSA algorithm, developed by Ron Rivest, Adi Shamir, and Leonard Adleman in 1977, became a hallmark of public-key cryptography. RSA relies on the mathematical difficulty of factoring large composite numbers to ensure the security of encrypted data. This algorithm paved the way for secure digital communication, e-commerce, and the widespread use of encryption on the internet.

While public-key cryptography brought newfound convenience and security, it also introduced new challenges. The management and distribution of public keys demanded trust and validation mechanisms, leading to the establishment of public-key infrastructures (PKIs).

One of the most transformative breakthroughs in modern cryptography was the development of public-key cryptography. In the 1970s, Whitfield Diffie and Martin Hellman introduced the concept of asymmetric encryption, where different keys are used for encryption and decryption.

Public-key cryptography revolutionized the field by providing a solution to the key distribution problem. The RSA algorithm, developed by Ronald Rivest, Adi Shamir, and Leonard Adleman in 1977, became the first practical implementation of public-key cryptography. It laid the foundation for secure digital communication, digital signatures, and secure electronic transactions.

Public-key cryptography opened the Pandora's box of data privacy. The ability to securely transmit and store sensitive information without a shared secret key transformed various industries, including finance, healthcare, and e-commerce. However, it also posed new challenges, as the robustness of encryption became a double-edged sword for law enforcement and national security agencies.

1.4.4 Navigating the Shifting Sands of Encryption Standards

The landscape of cryptography is continuously evolving, driven by advances in technology and the increasing sophistication of cyber threats. As cryptographic algorithms become more robust, adversaries, too, strive to exploit vulnerabilities.

The data encryption standard (DES), developed in the 1970s, was the first widely used encryption standard. However, as computing power increased, DES's 56-bit key length became susceptible to brute-force attacks. This led to the development of the advanced encryption standard (AES) in the early 2000s, with key lengths of 128, 192, or 256 bits, providing significantly higher security.

The need for continuous advancements in encryption standards is evident in the face of emerging technologies like quantum computing. Quantum computers, with their exponentially higher processing capabilities, pose a potential threat to classical cryptographic systems. As a result, researchers are exploring quantum-resistant algorithms that can withstand attacks from quantum adversaries.

In this chapter, we have explored the evolutionary path of modern cryptography, from the rudimentary ciphers of antiquity to the sophisticated algorithms of today. But as we embrace the transformative power of encryption, we must also be mindful of its consequences on humanity. In the following chapters, we shall delve deeper into the impact of cryptography on our society, exploring the human experience amidst a world governed by algorithms.

The evolution of modern cryptography showcases the transformative power of human innovation. From ancient ciphers to the RSA algorithm, cryptography has evolved to meet the ever-increasing demands for secure communication in the digital age.

Pioneers and revolutionary breakthroughs in the field have led to the development of encryption algorithms that protect our sensitive data and enable secure digital transactions. Public-key cryptography, in particular, has revolutionized the way we encrypt information, paving the way for secure communication and data privacy.

However, as we embrace the benefits of encryption, we must also confront the challenges it poses to law enforcement and national security. Striking a balance between privacy and public safety remains a complex task, requiring ongoing discussions and collaboration among technologists, policymakers, and society at large.

In the chapters that follow, we will delve deeper into the intricacies of modern cryptographic algorithms, explore the ethical implications of encryption, and navigate the evolving landscape of data privacy and security. Let us continue our exploration into the world of cryptography, unraveling its secrets and uncovering its impact on our digital lives.

Chapter 2

Evolution of Codes, Ciphers, and Cryptography

2.1 BRIEF HISTORY

From the dawn of civilization until now, codes, ciphers, and cryptography have been invented and utilized in myriad ways. It would be out of context to mention about its evolution in detail. However, a bird's-eye view is required in order to understand the purport of this book.

Next is a timeline highlighting key milestones and advancements in the evolution of cryptography:

- **1900 BCE:** The earliest known evidence of cryptography is found in the ancient Egyptian hieroglyphics, which show examples of simple substitution ciphers.

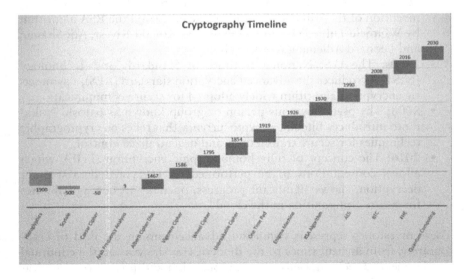

Figure 2.1 Evolution of Cryptography.

DOI: 10.1201/9781003527220-3

- **500 BCE:** The Spartan military uses the Scytale, a transposition cipher device, for secure communication.
- **50 BCE:** Julius Caesar develops the Caesar cipher, a substitution cipher, which involves shifting each letter of the alphabet a fixed number of positions.
- **9th century:** Arab scholars make significant contributions to cryptography, including the invention of frequency analysis, a technique to break substitution ciphers.
- **1467:** Leon Battista Alberti, an Italian philosopher and mathematician, introduces the Alberti Cipher Disk, a polyalphabetic cipher device.
- **1586:** Blaise de Vigenère, a French diplomat, develops the Vigenère cipher, a polyalphabetic substitution cipher that uses a keyword for encryption.
- **1795:** Thomas Jefferson designs the wheel cipher, a mechanical device used to encipher and decipher messages.
- **1854:** Charles Babbage, an English mathematician and inventor, proposes the concept of the "unbreakable" cipher, which later influences the development of modern cryptography.
- **1918–1919:** The American engineer Gilbert Vernam and army officer Joseph Mauborgne invent the one-time pad, a form of encryption using a random key that is only used once, making it theoretically unbreakable.
- **1926:** The German engineer Arthur Scherbius patents the Enigma machine, an electromechanical rotor cipher machine that becomes widely used by the military and intelligence agencies.
- **1970s:** The development of public-key cryptography begins, with the invention of the Diffie–Hellman key exchange and the RSA algorithm by Whitfield Diffie, Martin Hellman, and Ronald Rivest, Adi Shamir, and Leonard Adleman, respectively.
- **1990s:** The U.S. National Institute of Standards and Technology (NIST) introduces the advanced encryption standard (AES), a symmetric encryption algorithm widely adopted for secure communication.
- **2008:** The pseudonymous person or group known as Satoshi Nakamoto introduces Bitcoin, a cryptocurrency that relies on cryptographic techniques for secure transactions and decentralized control.
- **2016:** The concept of fully homomorphic encryption (FHE), which allows computations to be performed on encrypted data without decryption, shows significant progress, opening up new possibilities for secure computation in the cloud.

These milestones represent significant advancements in the field of cryptography, from ancient times to the modern era, showcasing the continual development of techniques to secure information and protect communication in an evolving digital world.

2.2 CRYPTOGRAPHY AROUND THE WORLD

One famous story on ancient secret communication is that of the Spartan military tactic known as the "Scytale."

During the height of the Spartan military prowess in ancient Greece, the Scytale was used as a means of secret communication between the military commanders and soldiers. It is said to have been employed during the Peloponnesian War (431–404 BCE).

The Scytale was a cylinder made of wood or metal, around which a strip of parchment or leather was wrapped. The sender of the secret message would write the message along the length of the strip, and then unwrap it from the Scytale. The resulting message would appear as a jumble of seemingly random letters. To decipher the message, the receiver had to possess an identically sized cylinder, allowing the parchment to be rewrapped. When the strip was wrapped around the correct-sized cylinder, the original message would become readable.

The Scytale worked based on the principle of transposition cipher, which rearranges the order of letters in a message rather than replacing them with different symbols. By using the Scytale, the Spartans were able to send messages securely, knowing that even if intercepted by enemies, the information would be indecipherable without the corresponding cylinder.

The Scytale is often regarded as one of the earliest recorded examples of cryptographic techniques used for secret communication. Its simplicity and effectiveness made it a powerful tool in maintaining the secrecy of military communications for the Spartans during their campaigns.

The history of ciphers and cryptography spans thousands of years, dating back to ancient civilizations where secret messages and encrypted communication were used for military, diplomatic, and personal purposes. The art of concealing information has evolved significantly over time, adapting to the advancements in technology and mathematics. Here's a detailed account of the fascinating journey of ciphers and cryptography across the world:

Figure 2.2 Scytale Cipher Scroll.

2.2.1 Ancient Ciphers and Early Cryptography

Ancient Mesopotamia: One of the earliest recorded instances of cryptography can be traced back to ancient Mesopotamia around 1900 BCE. Clay tablets discovered in the region showed the use of simple substitution ciphers where symbols were replaced with other symbols or numbers.

Ancient Egypt: Hieroglyphics, used in ancient Egypt, had some elements of cryptography. Scribes used various methods of encryption to protect sensitive information, particularly for religious texts and state secrets.

Ancient Greece: The ancient Greeks used a cipher device known as the "Skytale" around 400 BCE. It consisted of a long, narrow strip of parchment wound around a staff of a particular diameter. The message was written along the parchment, and when unwound from the staff of the correct diameter, the text became illegible, acting as a form of transposition cipher.

Julius Caesar's Cipher: In ancient Rome, Julius Caesar is famously known to have used a substitution cipher known as the "Caesar cipher" or "shift cipher." Each letter in the plaintext was shifted a fixed number of positions down the alphabet to create the ciphertext. Caesar's cipher, with a shift of 3, became one of the earliest examples of symmetric key cryptography.

2.2.2 Medieval Cryptography

Arab Scholars: During the Islamic Golden Age (8th to 14th centuries), Arab scholars made significant contributions to cryptography. Al-Kindi, an Arab polymath, wrote a book called "Risalah fi Istikhraj al-Mu'amma" ("Manuscript for the Deciphering Cryptographic Messages"), which discussed various techniques for breaking ciphers.

The Vigenère Cipher: In the 16th century, Blaise de Vigenère, a French diplomat and cryptographer, created the Vigenère cipher—a polyalphabetic substitution cipher that was considered unbreakable for several centuries. It used a keyword to determine different Caesar ciphers for each letter of the plaintext.

2.2.3 Cryptography in the Age of Enlightenment

Leon Battista Alberti: During the Renaissance, the Italian polymath Leon Battista Alberti introduced the "Alberti Cipher Disk." It allowed for the quick encryption and decryption of messages using polyalphabetic substitution.

The Great Cipher: In the 17th century, French cryptographers Antoine and Bonaventure Rossignol developed the "Great Cipher" for King

Louis XIV. It was a complex substitution cipher used for diplomatic and military communications and remained unbroken for over two centuries.

2.2.4 The Birth of Modern Cryptanalysis

Frequency Analysis: In the 9th century, Arab scholar Al-Kindi introduced the concept of frequency analysis. This technique involved analyzing the frequency of letters or symbols in the ciphertext to deduce the underlying pattern, eventually breaking the encryption.

Charles Babbage and the Kasiski Examination: In the 19th century, Charles Babbage and Friedrich Kasiski made significant contributions to cryptanalysis. Kasiski developed a method to break Vigenère ciphers by finding repeating patterns in the ciphertext.

2.2.5 World War II and Beyond

Enigma Machine: During World War II, the Germans used the Enigma machine, an electromechanical device, to encrypt military communications. British cryptanalysts, including Alan Turing and his team at Bletchley Park, successfully cracked the Enigma, significantly aiding the Allied war effort.

Modern Cryptography: With the advent of computers, cryptography evolved rapidly. The data encryption standard (DES) was developed in the 1970s, followed by the more secure advanced encryption standard (AES) in the 2000s. Public-key cryptography, pioneered by Whitfield Diffie and Martin Hellman in the 1970s, revolutionized secure communication over insecure channels.

Internet and Cryptography: The rise of the internet brought new challenges in securing digital communication. Secure Sockets Layer (SSL) and its successor Transport Layer Security (TLS) protocols were developed to ensure secure data transmission over the internet.

Today, cryptography plays a crucial role in securing our digital world, from protecting sensitive information online to enabling secure financial transactions and safeguarding national security. As technology continues to advance, the field of cryptography remains a dynamic and vital aspect of our interconnected world.

2.3 CODES AND CIPHERS IN INDIA

Cryptography, the art of secret writing, has played a pivotal role in safeguarding sensitive information throughout history. While modern cryptography has seen remarkable advancements, it is essential to acknowledge the ancient roots of this science. India, with its rich historical heritage, is known to have employed sophisticated cryptographic techniques dating back to ancient times. This section delves into the history of cryptography in ancient India, highlighting some prominent examples of its usage and exploring how its principles are relatable to modern cryptography and encryption.

2.3.1 Ancient India

Vedas and Samhitas: The earliest references to cryptography in India can be found in ancient texts like the Vedas and Samhitas (circa 1500–500 BCE). These texts mentioned techniques to hide information and encrypt messages using various methods of substitution and transposition ciphers. One such technique was "Sandhi", where certain letters or syllables were split and scattered throughout the text, making it challenging to decipher without the correct knowledge of recombination.

Kautilya's Arthashastra: Written by the ancient Indian strategist and economist Chanakya, also known as Kautilya, around the 4th century BCE, the Arthashastra includes references to cryptographic practices employed for espionage and statecraft. It mentions the use of codes and ciphers to convey secret messages. It contains references to several cryptographic methods, including "Vyūha," a strategic military formation that used encoded signals and formations to communicate securely during warfare.

2.3.2 Medieval India

The*Kama Sutra*: The *Kama Sutra*, a well-known ancient Indian text on love and relationships written by Vatsyayana around the 2nd century CE, includes references to secret writing techniques and methods for concealing messages. The "Atbash" cipher, a simple substitution cipher, was used in ancient India and is found mentioned in the *Kamasutra*. This cipher replaced each letter with its reverse in the alphabet, providing a basic level of encryption.

The Bahmani Sultanate: During the medieval period, Indian rulers, like the Bahmani Sultanate in the Deccan (14th to 16th centuries), used cryptographic methods for secure communication. They employed simple substitution ciphers and letter rearrangements to encode their messages.

2.3.3 The Mughal Era

Akbar's Cryptographic Department: Emperor Akbar (r. 1556–1605) established a specialized department for cryptography in his court.

This department developed and used various ciphers and cryptographic techniques to ensure secure communication among officials and spies.

2.3.4 British Colonial Era

European Influence: With the advent of British rule in India, European cryptographic methods started influencing Indian communication practices. The British introduced modern cryptographic techniques, including the use of cipher machines, to enhance security.

Independence Struggle: During India's fight for independence from British colonial rule, freedom fighters and leaders used various cryptographic methods to exchange secret messages, evade surveillance, and organize resistance against the colonial authorities.

2.3.5 Modern India

After Independence (1947): Post independence, India focused on building its cryptographic capabilities to safeguard national security. The Intelligence Bureau (IB) and the military adopted modern encryption techniques to protect sensitive information and communications.

The Indian Space Research Organisation (ISRO): India's space agency, ISRO, also employs cryptography to protect its satellite communication systems and sensitive data related to space missions.

Cybersecurity and E-Governance: In the modern era of digital transformation, India has prioritized cybersecurity and encryption for secure e-governance and digital communication across various government departments and organizations.

Aadhaar: The Indian government introduced the Aadhaar project, a unique biometric identification system for citizens, which also incorporates strong cryptographic protocols to ensure data privacy and security.

Indian Cryptographic Research and Development: India has seen advancements in cryptographic research and development. Several Indian institutions and organizations actively contribute to cryptographic protocols and algorithms.

Data Protection and Privacy Laws: In recent years, India has been working on data protection laws and privacy regulations that encompass the responsible use of encryption to safeguard personal information and sensitive data.

In retrospection, India's history of ciphers and cryptography spans centuries, with contributions from ancient texts, rulers, and modern researchers. From ancient times to the modern era, cryptography remains an essential tool for safeguarding information, ensuring secure communication, and protecting national interests in India and around the world.

Here are some key aspects of cryptography in India:

- **Classical Cryptography:** The ancient Indian texts known as the Vedas, dating back to around 1500 BCE, contain references to cryptographic techniques. The Rigveda mentions the use of codes and ciphers in concealing secret knowledge. Classical Indian texts, such as the *Kama Sutra* and the Arthashastra, also discuss encryption methods and their applications in secret communication.

- **Steganography:** Steganography, the art of hiding secret information within seemingly innocuous carriers, has a long history in India. One of the earliest known steganographic techniques was the "Madhya Rekha," or "Middle Line" method, where a hidden message was written in the middle of a seemingly ordinary text. The recipient would know to extract the concealed message by following specific instructions.

- **Kautilya's Arthashastra:** The Arthashastra, a treatise on governance and statecraft attributed to the ancient scholar Kautilya (also known as Chanakya), covers various aspects of administration, including cryptography. It discusses methods of encryption, decryption, and ensuring secure communication for military and political purposes.

- **The Kerala School of Mathematics:** The Kerala School of Mathematics, which flourished between the 14th and 16th centuries in southern India, made significant contributions to mathematics, including cryptography. Scholars like Nilakantha Somayaji developed encryption techniques for concealing mathematical proofs and concepts.

- **The Maratha Cipher:** During the 17th and 18th centuries, the Maratha Empire in western India employed a cipher known as the "Maratha Cipher" for secure communication. It involved substituting letters with corresponding numbers or symbols, making the messages unintelligible to those without the key.

- **Modern Cryptography:** In more recent times, India has contributed to modern cryptography. Pioneering work has been done by Indian mathematicians and computer scientists in areas such as encryption algorithms, cryptographic protocols, and secure communication systems.

Additionally, India has established organizations like the Centre for Development of Advanced Computing (CDAC) and the Indian Statistical Institute (ISI) that have been involved in cryptographic research and development. The Indian government has also formulated policies and regulations related to encryption to ensure secure communication and protect national security interests.

Cryptography continues to be an important field in India, with ongoing research, innovation, and applications in areas such as cybersecurity, secure communication, and data protection.

2.3.6 The Atbash Cipher

The Atbash cipher, a simple substitution cipher, has a long history and finds mention in ancient Indian texts, including the famous *Kamasutra*. This cryptographic technique served as a means to conceal sensitive information, particularly in the context of the intimate and secretive nature of the *Kamasutra*.

2.3.6.1 The Atbash Cipher in the Kamasutra

The *Kamasutra*, attributed to the ancient Indian scholar Vatsyayana, is a revered text on human relationships, love, and intimacy. Among its varied topics, the *Kamasutra* also touches upon the art of secret communication through the application of the Atbash cipher. The Atbash cipher is a monoalphabetic substitution cipher, meaning it replaces each letter of the plaintext with a corresponding letter from the end of the alphabet.

2.3.6.2 Working Principles of the Atbash Cipher

The Atbash cipher follows a straightforward substitution pattern. Each letter in the plaintext is replaced with its mirror image in the alphabet. For instance, "A" becomes "Z", "B" becomes "Y", "C" becomes "X", and so on. The decryption process is identical to encryption, making it a symmetric encryption technique.

For example, the word "LOVE" in the Atbash cipher would be encrypted as "OLHV", and decrypting "OLHV" would yield "LOVE".

2.3.6.3 Relativity to Advanced Encryption System (AES)

While the Atbash cipher was a rudimentary cryptographic method used in ancient India, it shares some fundamental concepts with the modern AES.

2.3.6.4 Substitution Cipher

Both the Atbash cipher and AES operate on the principle of substitution. The Atbash cipher substitutes each letter with another letter based on a fixed rule, while AES, an advanced symmetric encryption algorithm, substitutes plaintext blocks with corresponding ciphertext blocks using a complex key-dependent process.

2.3.6.5 Symmetric Key Encryption

The Atbash cipher and AES are both symmetric key encryption techniques. In the Atbash cipher, the same key is used for both encryption and decryption. Similarly, AES employs a symmetric key for both encryption and decryption operations. This means that the same secret key is used by both parties to secure their communication.

2.3.6.6 Encryption Complexity

Unlike AES, the Atbash cipher lacks complexity and security features necessary for modern cryptographic needs. The Atbash cipher's simplicity makes it vulnerable to modern computational attacks, such as frequency analysis, which allows adversaries to deduce the encryption key and decrypt the message easily. AES, on the other hand, is highly robust and widely adopted due to its complex mathematical operations, making it computationally infeasible to reverse engineer the encryption key.

2.3.6.7 Historical Significance

While the Atbash cipher holds historical significance and provides a glimpse into ancient cryptographic practices, AES represents the pinnacle of modern encryption technology. AES is the standard encryption algorithm used worldwide for securing sensitive information, including financial transactions, military communications, and digital data.

The Atbash cipher, an ancient Indian cryptographic technique used in the *Kamasutra*, demonstrates the early human fascination with secret communication and encryption. Although simple and historically relevant, the Atbash cipher lacks the sophistication and security features required to protect sensitive data in the modern era. In contrast, the advanced encryption system (AES) is a highly advanced and widely adopted encryption algorithm that ensures robust security in digital communications. By examining the Atbash cipher's historical context and its comparison to AES, we gain a deeper understanding of the evolution of cryptography, from ancient India to the technologically advanced present.

2.3.7 Ardhamagadhi Prakrit Cipher

One intriguing ancient Indian story related to codes and ciphers is the tale of the "Ardhamagadhi Prakrit Cipher".

The Ardhamagadhi Prakrit Cipher story is associated with Emperor Ashoka, who ruled over the Mauryan Empire in India during the 3rd century BCE. Ashoka was known for his extensive use of edicts and inscriptions, spreading his messages and policies across the empire. However, some

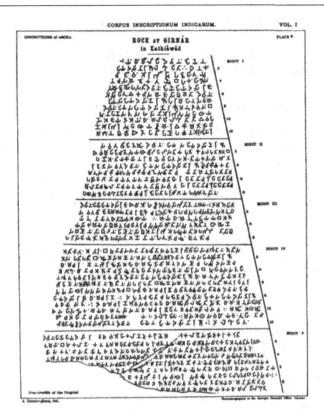

Figure 2.3 Ardhamagadhi Prakrit Cipher Tablet.

of these inscriptions were written in a cryptic cipher known as Ardhamagadhi Prakrit.

According to the story, Emperor Ashoka devised the Ardhamagadhi Prakrit Cipher as a way to encode secret messages, enabling confidential communication between trusted individuals within his administration. The cipher involved replacing individual characters or syllables with specific symbols or combinations of symbols, rendering the text incomprehensible to anyone who did not possess the key to decipher it.

It is said that Ashoka employed this cipher to send covert messages to his spies, military commanders, and administrators throughout the vast empire. By using the cipher, Ashoka ensured that his instructions remained confidential and that sensitive information would not fall into the wrong hands.

The Ardhamagadhi Prakrit Cipher story demonstrates the ancient Indian understanding of the importance of encryption and secrecy in communication. It highlights the strategic use of ciphers to protect sensitive information and maintain secure channels of communication within the empire. While the exact details of the cipher are not widely known or documented, the story serves as a testament to the ancient Indian ingenuity in employing codes and ciphers for covert communication purposes.

2.3.8 Kutila Samvad

Another fascinating ancient Indian story related to codes and ciphers is the tale of the "Kutila Samvad". The Kutila Samvad, meaning "Clever Dialogue" or "Ingenious Conversation", is an ancient Indian text that describes a conversation between two characters, Kutila and Samayaka. In this story, Kutila, a minister or advisor, imparts wisdom to Samayaka, the king's son, through a series of encrypted messages.

The encrypted messages in the Kutila Samvad are constructed using various cryptographic techniques, including substitution, transposition, and wordplay. Kutila presents puzzles, riddles, and hidden meanings within his messages, challenging Samayaka to decipher them and extract the hidden knowledge and advice they contain.

Kutila says:

य एवादिः स एवान्तो मध्ये भवति मध्यमः |
य एतन्नाभिजानीयात् तृणमात्रं न वेत्ति सः ||

Direct / literal meaning:

Its beginning is its end. Its middle is its middle. If you don't know this, you don't know anything.

Another interpretation:

It starts with "ya" and ends with "sa", in the middle is a semivowel. If you don't know this, you don't know even a blade of grass.

Samayaka answers:

यवस

It starts with य and ends with स. In the middle is the semivowel व. यवस means a blade of grass.

The answer is actually hidden surreptitiously in the question itself. The reader is misled because य and स are also pronouns.

The story showcases the use of ciphers and encrypted communication as a means of conveying important information discreetly and promoting intellectual stimulation. It underscores the ancient Indian fascination with codes, puzzles, and the art of deciphering messages, highlighting the importance of cryptology as a tool for education, problem-solving, and transmitting secret knowledge.

The Kutila Samvad is an intriguing testament to the long-standing tradition of cryptology and secret communication in ancient Indian culture. It exemplifies the Indian ingenuity in developing sophisticated encryption techniques and demonstrates the significance of codes and ciphers as vehicles for intellectual exchange and imparting wisdom.

2.3.9 Vedic "Katapayadi" Code

It is often known as the "KaTaPaYaDi Sutra". The following Vedic Numerical code was used in many slokas in ancient days:

कादि नव, टादि नव, पादि पञ्चक,
यद्यष्टक क्ष शुन्यम्,

"Kaadi nava, Taadi nava, Paadi panchaka,
Yadyashtaka Kshah sunyam"

Meaning:

Starting from ka, the sequence of 9 letters represent 1,2,..9. Similarly starting from ta, starting from pa, starting from ya and ksha represents 0.

In detail:

ka (क)-1, kha (ख)-2, ga (ग)-3, gha (घ)-4, gna (ङ)-5, cha (च)-6, cha (छ)-7, ja (ज)-8, jha (झ)-9

ta (ट)-1, tha (ठ)-2, da (ड)-3, dha (ढ)-4,~na (ण)-5, Ta (त)-6, Tha (थ)-7, Da (द)-8, Dha (ध)-9

pa (प)-1, pha (फ)-2, ba (ब)-3, bha (भ)-4, ma (म)-5

ya (य)-1, ra (र)-2, la (ल)-3, va (व)-4, Sa (श)-5, sha (ष)-6, sa (स)-7, ha (ह)-8

kshah (क्ष)-0.

Based on this code there are many slokas in mathematics. Following is a sloka for pi value:

गोपीभाग्य मधुव्रातः श्रृंगशोदधि संधिगः |
खलजीवितखाताव गलहाला रसंधरः ||

gopeebhaagya maDhuvraathaH shruMgashodhaDhi saMDhigaH
khalajeevithakhaathaava galahaalaa rasaMDharaH

ga-3, pa-1, bha-4, ya -1, ma-5, Dhu-9, ra-2, tha-6, shru-5, ga-3, sho-5, dha-8, Dhi -9, sa-7, Dha- 9, ga-3, kha-2, la-3, jee-8, vi-4, tha-6, kha-2, tha-6, va-4, ga-3, la-3, ha-8, la-3, ra-2, sa-7, Dha-9, ra-2

3.14159265358979323846264338327 92. . .

The previous sloka actually has three meanings:

1. In favor of Lord Shiva
2. In favor of Lord Krishna
3. The value of pi up to 32 decimals.

There were many inventions in the field of science and technology in ancient India, we just have to sift through the sands of time to find them.

Cryptography in ancient India demonstrates the early human quest for secure communication and knowledge preservation. The techniques employed during that time laid the groundwork for many concepts that are still applicable in modern cryptographic practices. The shared principles of secrecy, algorithmic complexity, key-based encryption, and secure key management demonstrate the enduring relevance of ancient Indian cryptography to modern encryption systems. By understanding the historical roots of cryptography, we gain valuable insights into the evolution of data security and encryption, leading to more robust and advanced techniques in the digital age.

2.4 RELATABILITY OF ANCIENT INDIAN CIPHERS

Ancient ciphers and modern cryptography differ significantly in terms of complexity, security, and the technology used. However, ancient Indian ciphers have much in common with encryption techniques being used today.

2.4.1 Shared Principles

Several principles in ancient Indian cryptography remain applicable in modern encryption techniques. For instance, the notion of key-based encryption was present in classical Indian ciphers. Just as modern encryption relies on keys for encoding and decoding data, ancient Indian ciphers also required specific keys or knowledge of certain rules for decryption.

2.4.2 Algorithmic Complexity

Ancient Indian cryptographic techniques often relied on algorithmic complexity to enhance security. For example, the "Sandhi" technique scattered syllables throughout texts, making it laborious for unauthorized individuals to reassemble the original message. Similarly, modern encryption algorithms, such as the advanced encryption standard (AES), use complex mathematical operations that are computationally infeasible to reverse without the correct key.

2.4.3 Secrecy and Steganography

The concept of keeping cryptographic methods secret was vital in ancient India, as it is in modern times. Storing encrypted messages in innocuous carriers, a form of steganography, was also practiced to evade detection by adversaries. Today, steganography remains an integral part of digital cryptography, where data can be concealed within images, audio, or video files.

2.4.4 Key Management and Distribution

Ancient Indian cryptography highlights the significance of secure key management and distribution. For cryptographic techniques to be effective, the keys must be known only to authorized parties. This principle resonates strongly in modern cryptography, where secure key exchange protocols, like Diffie–Hellman, are used to establish shared secrets over insecure communication channels.

2.5 COMPARISON OF ANCIENT V/S MODERN

Now, let us compare the ancient ciphers used worldwide with modern cryptography as it is.

Table 2.1 Cipher v/s. Cryptography.

Factors	Ancient Ciphers	Modern Cryptography
Complexity	were relatively simple and often relied on basic substitution or transposition techniques. Examples include Caesar cipher (substitution), Skytale (transposition), and Vigenère cipher (polyalphabetic substitution). These ciphers were relatively easy to understand and implement.	involves highly complex algorithms and mathematical principles. It encompasses both symmetric-key cryptography (where the same key is used for encryption and decryption) and public-key cryptography (where different keys are used for encryption and decryption). Advanced encryption algorithms like AES (advanced encryption standard) and RSA (Rivest–Shamir–Adleman) are widely used, and breaking them requires significant computational power and time.

(Continued)

Table 2.1 (Continued)

Factors	Ancient Ciphers	Modern Cryptography
Security	Most ancient ciphers lacked strong security, and many of them were vulnerable to cryptanalysis. With limited complexity, they could be easily broken through simple frequency analysis, letter distribution, or by exploiting known patterns.	algorithms are designed to be highly secure and resistant to various attacks, including brute-force attacks, differential cryptanalysis, and known-plaintext attacks. The security of modern cryptography is based on the difficulty of solving complex mathematical problems, such as factoring large numbers (RSA) or searching for specific patterns (AES).
Key Management	Key management was relatively straightforward since most ciphers used a single secret key for both encryption and decryption. The challenge was often in securely communicating the key to the recipient.	Key management is a critical aspect of modern cryptography. For symmetric-key cryptography, distributing and managing secret keys securely can be a significant challenge, especially when dealing with multiple users and systems. Public-key cryptography provides an elegant solution to key distribution but introduces other challenges, such as the need for a public-key infrastructure (PKI).
Technology	were primarily implemented using manual methods, such as writing on parchment, using physical devices like the Skytale, or creating simple mechanical devices for substitution.	relies heavily on computer technology. Encryption and decryption processes are performed using algorithms implemented in software or hardware. Cryptographic keys are generated, stored, and managed digitally. The use of computers enables faster and more efficient cryptographic operations.
Scope of Use	were limited in scope and often used for specific purposes, such as protecting military messages, secret communication among rulers and officials, or concealing sensitive information in religious texts.	It is used extensively in secure communication over the internet (e.g., HTTPS), protecting sensitive data in databases, securing financial transactions, digital signatures, securing mobile communication, and ensuring the integrity of software and hardware through digital signatures and code signing.

In summary, while ancient ciphers were historically significant and laid the groundwork for cryptography, modern cryptography has evolved into a highly sophisticated field, with complex algorithms, robust security, and versatile applications in our digitally connected world. The shift from manual methods to computer-based encryption has dramatically improved the security and effectiveness of cryptographic systems.

Chapter 3

Man v/s. Machine

3.1 PERSPECTIVES

Figure 3.1 Lifting Equipment.

DOI: 10.1201/9781003527220-4   45

Just because a man can't lift 10,000 tons but a man-made crane can, does that make—

1. Crane stronger than man?
2. Crane more important than man?
3. Crane better than man?

To add to the context, modern computers are built on the concept of bio-mimicry. In fact, the McCullogh–Pittz artificial neuron is exactly a copy

Figure 3.2 Modern Computers.

of how natural neurons are fired and form networks inside our brains. For the layman, here's the basic list of operations carried out by artificial neurons:

- Comprehension—most algorithms are dedicated for context, comparison, and calibration
- Cut, Copy, and Paste—data acquisition, sorting, and analysis
- Fill in the Blanks—generating the desired response
- Match the Following—labeling, supervised / unsupervised learning
- True or False—similar to the previous but a bit more complex

So then, why are Turing-complete machines (read computers, robots, etc., that run on algorithms) considered to be a competition for mankind?

If not, then there is no question of "Technological singularity" at all. It's all a hoax just like the "Mechanical Turkman". We will discuss more on this in the next chapter.

In the current scenario, where we are all witnessing concerted efforts to project an apparent reality while the truth is otherwise, we need to analyze the possible outcomes.

To be able to do this, we need to be able to visualize different perspectives.

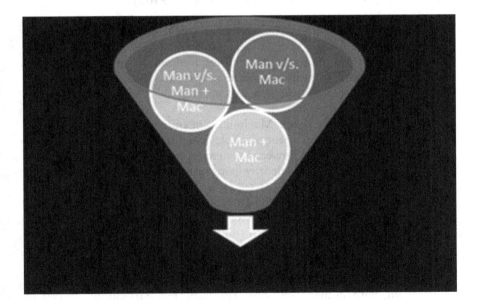

Figure 3.3 Man or Machine.

3.1.1 Apparent Reality: Man v/s Machine

Is this really the truth? Have we truly reached a level where AI and other emerging technologies are about to surpass human beings in their collective endeavor?

3.1.2 The Reality: Man v/s (Man + Machine)

Maybe we need to have another look at the prevailing scenario. It might just be a case of men without machines pitted against men with machines. Is it about an uneven field, where the one who isn't equipped with the latest technologies is bound to be conquered or eliminated?

3.1.3 Ideal Goal: Man + Machine

All machines are man-made after all and their purpose is to serve mankind. They are not at all meant to compete with or displace humans but instead augment our collective abilities. Just because a crane can lift a hundred tons, while a man cannot, doesn't make it a challenger to mankind. Then, why this scare about AI surpassing humans?

3.2 APPARENT REALITY: CONSUMERIST PROJECTION

The "man versus machine" scenario refers to the concept of humans pitted against artificial intelligence or advanced machines in various domains. It often raises questions about the capabilities, limitations, and potential consequences of technology surpassing human abilities. Here are a few aspects to consider in the man versus machine scenario:

- **Expertise and Efficiency:** Machines can outperform humans in specific tasks that require speed, accuracy, and processing vast amounts of data. For instance, AI-powered systems can analyze complex datasets, make predictions, and identify patterns with greater efficiency than humans.
- **Creativity and Intuition:** While machines excel in tasks driven by data and algorithms, human creativity and intuition remain unparalleled. Humans possess the ability to think abstractly, find innovative solutions, and bring a unique perspective that machines cannot replicate.
- **Emotional Intelligence and Empathy:** Machines lack emotional intelligence and empathy, which are essential for understanding and connecting with human emotions. This aspect is particularly crucial in fields like healthcare, counseling, and interpersonal interactions.
- **Ethical Considerations:** The deployment of advanced machines raises ethical questions. Ensuring that machines make unbiased decisions,

adhere to ethical guidelines, and consider human values requires careful design, oversight, and accountability.

- **Collaboration and Complementarity:** The most effective approach is often a collaboration between humans and machines, leveraging the strengths of each. Machines can assist humans in decision-making, data analysis, and performing repetitive tasks, while humans can provide contextual understanding, critical thinking, and ethical judgment.
- **Potential Impact on Jobs:** The rise of automation and AI has sparked concerns about job displacement. While machines can automate routine tasks, they also create new opportunities and jobs that require human skills such as creativity, problem-solving, and emotional intelligence.
- **Human–Machine Interface:** Developing intuitive and user-friendly interfaces between humans and machines is essential for effective collaboration and adoption. Advancements in natural language processing, gesture recognition, and augmented reality can enhance human–machine interaction.

It's important to approach the man versus machine scenario as an opportunity for collaboration and augmentation, rather than a binary competition. By leveraging the strengths of both humans and machines, we can achieve outcomes that are more efficient, innovative, and beneficial for society as a whole.

3.3 THE REALITY: ISOLATION

3.3.1 The Dark Side of Convenience: Erosion of Human Interaction

In the digital age, technology has bestowed upon us unprecedented convenience and connectivity. We can communicate instantaneously with loved ones across continents, conduct business transactions with a few taps on a screen, and access a wealth of information at our fingertips. Modern cryptography plays a pivotal role in enabling this convenience by securing our digital interactions and safeguarding our personal data.

Yet, amidst the allure of seamless communication lies a paradox—a subtle erosion of human interaction. The virtual realm, with its anonymity and detachment, often replaces the warmth of face-to-face conversations and genuine connections. The ease of remote communication may inadvertently diminish the value of meaningful interactions, leaving us yearning for authentic human contact.

As modern cryptography enables seamless digital communication and transactions, it also presents a paradoxical challenge—the erosion of human interaction in the pursuit of convenience. In the digital age, individuals often find themselves communicating through text messages, emails, and social media platforms, replacing face-to-face conversations.

While digital communication offers unparalleled speed and convenience, it can create a sense of detachment and disconnection. Emoticons may attempt to convey emotions, but they can never fully replace the nuances of in-person communication. The convenience of encryption-secured messaging may shield conversations from prying eyes, but it can also distance us from the empathy and understanding that human interactions provide.

3.3.2 Internet Surveillance and Privacy Concerns

As our lives intertwine with the digital landscape, we leave behind trails of data—our digital footprints—that are continuously monitored, collected, and analyzed. Governments, corporations, and malicious actors capitalize on this treasure trove of information, transforming the promise of convenience into a potential dystopia of surveillance.

The revelations by whistleblowers like Edward Snowden exposed widespread government surveillance programs, shaking the foundations of trust between citizens and their governing bodies. Surveillance mechanisms, ostensibly designed to bolster national security, have raised profound ethical and moral questions about the delicate balance between protecting society and preserving individual privacy.

The digital revolution has enabled governments and corporations to amass vast amounts of data about individuals, raising concerns about internet surveillance and privacy. Online activities, browsing habits, and social media interactions contribute to the creation of extensive digital profiles.

The pervasiveness of surveillance poses a challenge to individual privacy, as personal data becomes susceptible to misuse or exploitation. The collection and analysis of such data can lead to targeted advertising, personalized content, and, in some cases, potential manipulation of public opinion.

As we navigate the digital landscape, striking a balance between security and privacy is essential. Encryption technologies play a vital role in safeguarding individual data from unauthorized access. However, responsible data practices and transparent privacy policies are equally crucial to protect individuals from unwarranted surveillance.

3.3.3 The Perils of Digital Footprints and Data Breaches

While encryption is meant to safeguard our digital footprints, it cannot protect us from all threats. Data breaches, hacking incidents, and cyberattacks continue to pose serious risks to our personal and financial information. Despite sophisticated cryptographic measures, the human factor—lapses in security practices and social engineering—remains a significant vulnerability.

Data breaches can have far-reaching consequences, from financial losses and identity theft to reputational damage and emotional distress. The scale and frequency of such incidents underscore the ongoing struggle to reconcile the promises of modern cryptography with the realities of a digitized world.

Every digital interaction leaves behind a trail of data, creating digital footprints that can be exploited in unforeseen ways. Data breaches, cyberattacks, and hacking incidents pose significant risks to individuals and organizations alike.

The compromise of sensitive data can lead to identity theft, financial fraud, and reputational damage. Cybercriminals target personal information, financial records, and even medical data, exploiting vulnerabilities in data security.

The implications of data breaches extend beyond individuals, affecting public trust in institutions and corporations. The erosion of trust due to data breaches can have far-reaching consequences for the economy and society at large.

3.3.4 Cryptography, Identity, and Digital Personhood

In the interconnected web of the digital landscape, our identities have taken on new dimensions. Our online personas, shaped by our digital activities and interactions, become part of our modern identity. Cryptography is instrumental in maintaining the integrity and security of these digital personae, protecting them from manipulation and exploitation.

However, the reliance on cryptographic systems also raises questions about the authenticity and trustworthiness of digital identities. As deepfake technology and sophisticated social engineering attacks emerge, distinguishing genuine digital personas from manipulated ones becomes increasingly challenging.

3.3.5 The Human Element in Encryption

As we navigate the virtual realm, the human element in encryption becomes both a strength and a weakness. Human errors in key management and cryptographic practices can inadvertently lead to security breaches. Moreover, the psychological implications of living in a world governed by cryptography cannot be ignored.

The constant awareness of surveillance and the fear of cyberattacks give rise to "cybersecurity anxiety", a sense of vulnerability and helplessness in the face of ever-present digital threats. Understanding the emotional aspects of cryptography is crucial as we seek to strike a harmonious balance between technology and human well-being.

In this chapter, we have explored the technological mirage that surrounds modern cryptography. The allure of convenience and security coexists with the perils of surveillance and vulnerability. As we continue to navigate this complex landscape, we must not forget the human dimension—the emotions, interactions, and digital identities that shape our experience in the digital realm. In the forthcoming chapters, we shall delve deeper into the social and ethical implications of cryptography, unraveling the intricate relationship between technology and humanity.

The technological mirage of modern cryptography presents both opportunities and challenges. The convenience of digital communication and secure transactions revolutionizes the way we interact and conduct business. However, it also brings to light concerns regarding the erosion of human interaction, internet surveillance, and data privacy.

As we navigate the digital landscape, we must strike a balance between leveraging encryption technologies to protect our digital interactions while preserving human connection and empathy. Responsible data practices, transparent privacy policies, and ethical use of technology will be key in safeguarding individual privacy and building trust in the digital realm.

In the chapters that follow, we will delve deeper into the ethical implications of cryptography, explore the complexities of data privacy and security, and seek to understand the responsibilities of individuals, corporations, and governments in shaping a digital future that prioritizes both convenience and human values. Let us continue our exploration, peering beyond the technological mirage, and uncovering the profound impact of modern cryptography on our digital lives.

3.4 IDEAL GOAL: SIMPLE ETHICAL MACHINES

3.4.1 Balancing Human Needs and Technological Advancements

Anthropocentric information technology refers to the design, development, and deployment of technology with a primary focus on fulfilling human needs and enhancing the human experience. It is an approach that acknowledges the central role of humans in the technological landscape, prioritizing their well-being, values, and ethical considerations. In an era of rapid technological advancement, adopting an anthropocentric perspective becomes essential to ensure that technology serves human interests while mitigating potential negative impacts.

3.4.2 Empowering Humans through Technology

Anthropocentric information technology aims to empower individuals and societies by leveraging technology to improve various aspects of human life. From communication to healthcare, education to entertainment, and beyond, technology is harnessed to enhance human capabilities, foster innovation, and enable personal growth. User-centered design principles are employed to create intuitive interfaces, accessible applications, and seamless interactions, ensuring that technology is user friendly and adaptable to diverse user needs.

3.4.3 Enhancing Efficiency and Productivity

Anthropocentric information technology strives to optimize workflow, streamline processes, and increase efficiency in various domains. Automation, artificial intelligence, and machine learning are employed to assist humans in repetitive tasks, data analysis, decision-making, and problem-solving. By offloading mundane and time-consuming activities to machines, individuals can focus on more creative and strategic endeavors, leading to higher productivity and improved work–life balance.

3.4.4 Improving Quality of Life

Information technology plays a pivotal role in improving the quality of life for individuals and communities. From smart homes that enhance comfort and convenience to assistive technologies that support people with disabilities, technology-driven solutions are designed to cater to specific needs and enhance overall well-being. Advancements in healthcare technology, such as telemedicine and wearable devices, enable remote monitoring, personalized treatments, and early disease detection, contributing to improved health outcomes.

3.4.5 Social Impact and Connectivity

Anthropocentric information technology promotes connectivity and social interactions by bridging geographical, cultural, and social gaps. Social media platforms, messaging apps, and online communities facilitate global communication, collaboration, and knowledge sharing, fostering social connections and the exchange of diverse perspectives. However, it is crucial to strike a balance between virtual interactions and real-world relationships to ensure that technology does not hinder genuine human connections.

3.4.6 Ethical Considerations and Human Values

An anthropocentric approach to information technology acknowledges the ethical implications and human values associated with technological advancements. It calls for the responsible and ethical use of technology, considering privacy, security, fairness, and transparency. It also emphasizes the need to mitigate biases in algorithms, address algorithmic discrimination, and ensure the ethical use of emerging technologies such as artificial intelligence and biometrics.

3.4.7 Sustainability and Environmental Impact

An anthropocentric perspective extends beyond human-centric concerns and encompasses the environmental impact of technology. Recognizing the importance of ecological balance and sustainability, information technology is leveraged to develop energy-efficient solutions, reduce carbon footprints, and promote eco-friendly practices. Cloud computing, virtualization, and energy-efficient hardware design contribute to minimizing the environmental impact of technology infrastructure.

Anthropocentric information technology puts humans at the center of technological development, focusing on meeting human needs, enhancing capabilities, and preserving human values. By adopting this approach, technology becomes a powerful tool for empowering individuals, improving efficiency, and enhancing the overall quality of life. However, it is crucial to strike a balance between technological advancements and ethical considerations, sustainability, and the preservation of genuine human connections. By embracing an anthropocentric perspective, we can harness the potential of technology to create a future that aligns with human aspirations while fostering a harmonious relationship between humans and the digital world.

3.4.8 Embracing Ethical Cryptography—Paving the Way for a Harmonious Future

In the ever-evolving digital landscape, the profound impact of cryptography on humanity calls for a thoughtful and ethical approach to technology. Our journey through the history, challenges, and ethical dimensions of modern cryptography has illuminated the delicate balance between security imperatives and human values.

As we embrace the concept of ethical cryptography, we find ourselves standing at the threshold of a harmonious future—a future where technology serves as a force for good, upholding privacy, individual rights, and democratic principles.

Privacy stands as a fundamental human right, and ethical cryptography empowers individuals with personal agency over their data and digital identities. By prioritizing privacy by design and resisting surveillance overreach, we can foster an environment where individuals feel confident expressing themselves freely without fear of unwarranted intrusion.

Digital literacy and inclusivity will be the bedrock of this harmonious future. Empowering individuals with the knowledge and skills to navigate the digital landscape responsibly bridges the digital divide, enabling marginalized communities to participate fully in the digital realm without compromising their privacy or safety.

Responsible innovation, collaboration, and transparent policy-making are essential to forging this future. By transcending geopolitical boundaries and prioritizing global challenges, we can craft cryptographic policies that protect public safety while preserving human rights and democratic values.

Technology companies, as guardians of user data, play a pivotal role in shaping this harmonious future. By prioritizing privacy, transparency, and accountability, they can act as a moral compass in the digital landscape, earning and maintaining user trust.

Our exploration into the intricate world of cryptography has shown us that the future is not predetermined; it is a collective creation—an intricate synthesis of technology and humanity. As we navigate this digital frontier, we must do so with a deep sense of responsibility and a commitment to human values.

Ethical cryptography invites us to envision a world where technology aligns with the best interests of humanity. It beckons us to weave a fabric that embraces privacy, empowers individuals, and elevates human dignity.

Together, we can shape a world where ethical cryptography becomes the foundation of a digital landscape that celebrates our diversity, respects our rights, and empowers us to thrive in a world of endless possibilities.

As we step into this harmonious future, let us carry with us the wisdom gained from our exploration. Let us embrace the ethical imperative that beckons us to forge a path of responsible innovation, collaboration, and user-centric design.

In the harmonious synthesis of technology and humanity lies the promise of a future where technology serves human values, and our digital journey becomes a testament to the greatness of our shared human spirit.

3.5 INCONGRUITIES WITH INFORMATION SECURITY

Data losses are not new and are as old as the human civilization itself. However, the way infosec has developed rapidly in the past few decades, by now we should have reached 6-sigma level of performance, i.e., 3.4 DPMO (defects per million opportunities). Alas, the truth is otherwise. I will demonstrate the reality with facts in the following paragraphs.

3.5.1 Overview of Data Breaches

Data losses did not merely begin with the advent of the digital era, but has roots during prehistoric eras too. Have a look at ancient data losses throughout history:

Table 3.1 Ancient Data Breach.

S. No.	Data Breach	Date	Records Lost*	Description
1	The Royal Library of Ashurbanipal	600 BC	13.71 GB	12,000 tablets affected in the sacking of Nineveh
2	The Library of Alexandria	48 BC	571.42 GB	500,000 scrolls lost in a fire during Caesar's civil war
3	Takshashila Vidyapith	5th century CE	Unknown	Several manuscripts on various subjects destroyed by invader Kidara Huns
4	Nalanda Mahavira	1193 AD	13.45 TB	9,000,000 manuscripts on several subjects burnt by Mughal chieftain Bakhtiyar Khilji
5	Vikramshila Mahavira	1193 AD	Unknown	Several manuscripts on various subjects destroyed by Mughal chieftain Bakhtiyar Khilji
6	Vallabhi Vidyapith	12th century CE	Unknown	Slowly declined after defeat of Maitraka Kingdom
7	Kanthalloor Shala	12th CE	Unknown	Slowly declined after defeat of Aayi Kingdom
8	The Maya Religious Codices	1562 AD	22.99 GB	20,040 religious codices destroyed by Spanish conquistadors

*Estimated data size is as per computer forensics investigation techniques based on archaeological facts or historical anecdotes

The previous table is evidence enough that data loss in large amounts during ancient times occurred due to wars and human errors. The scenario hasn't changed much in our modern times since major data losses still occur due to human errors and malwares (read: *cyberwarfare*).

In the digital world, a data breach may occur in one of the four typical methods:

- Ransomware
- Malware
- Phishing
- Denial-Of-Service

More on this is provided in Chapter 12: "Technical Notes". Interested readers can jump to that chapter if they are unable to understand these terms and are unable to do further reading right away.

If you are an IT practitioner, you must be aware of the top ten cybersecurity breaches of all time. However, the top hundred data breaches have occurred in the last one and a half decades alone. As of 2022, 15+ million global data records have been exposed, leaked, or lost. Here's a collection of the top 125 data breaches in the last two decades:

Table 3.2 Modern Data Breaches.

S. No.	Data Breach	Year (Breach / Disclosure)	Records Lost (Estimates)	Data Type
Top 30 Data Breaches till 2022				
1	CAM4	2020	10,880,000,000	Customer data, PII, sensitive info
2	Yahoo!	2013/17	3,000,000,000	Customer info
3	River City Media	2017	1,370,000,000	Email data backup
4	Aadhaar	2018	1,100,000,000	Biometric database of Indians
5	Alibaba.com	2022	1,100,000,000	Customer data, PII
6	First American	2019	885,000,000	Financial info, PII, sensitive data
7	Verifications.io	2019	763,000,000	Email addresses, PII
8	Spambot	2017	711,000,000	Emails and passwords
9	LinkedIn	2021	700,000,000	Data leak of user info
10	16 Hacked Websites	2019	617,000,000	User accounts from 16 websites
11	Facebook	2019/21	533,000,000	User records
12	Syniverse	2021	500,000,000	PII, TSP data, sensitive information
13	Yahoo!	2014/16	500,000,000	User records
14	Starwood (Marriott International)	2014/18	500,000,000	Customer info, PII, sensitive data
15	MySpace	2016	427,000,000	User records
16	Adult Friend Finder Network	2016	412,000,000	User records
17	Exactis	2018	340,000,000	US Adults and Businesses, PII
18	Twitter	2018	338,000,000	User records
19	MongoDB	2019	275,000,000	PII of Indian citizens
20	Microsoft	2019	250,000,000	Customer service and support records
21	NetEase	2015	234,000,000	Email addresses and passwords
22	Chinese Job Websites (Socialarks.com)	2018/21	202,000,000	Jobseeker data, PII
23	Court Ventures	2013	200,000,000	PII of Americans
24	Deep Root Analytics	2015	198,000,000	US voter info
25	LinkedIn	2012	167,000,000	User records
26	DubSmash	2018	162,000,000	Email addresses and password hashes

(Continued)

Table 3.2 (Continued)

S. No.	Data Breach	Year (Breach / Disclosure)	Records Lost (Estimates)	Data Type
27	Multiple American Businesses	2019	160,000,000	Credit / debit card numbers of customers
28	Adobe	2013	152,000,000	User data
29	MyFitnessPal	2018	150,000,000	User data, PII
30	eBay	2014	145,000,000	User records

Rest of Top 125 Data Breaches till 2022

S. No.	Data Breach	Year (Breach / Disclosure)	Records Lost (Estimates)	Data Type
31	Equifax	2017	143,000,000	PII
32	Canva	2019	137,000,000	User data, PII
33	Heartland Payment Systems	2009	130,000,000	Payroll customer data
34	8 Hacked Websites	2019	127,000,000	User data
35	Apollo	2018	126,000,000	User data, PII
36	Badoo	2013	112,000,000	User data
37	Capital One	2019	106,000,000	PII
38	Evite	2013	101,000,000	User data, PII
39	Quora	2018	100,000,000	User data, PII
40	VK	2012	93,000,000	User data
41	MyHeritage	2018	92,000,000	User data, PII
42	YouKu	2016	92,000,000	User data
43	Rambler	2014	91,000,000	User data, PII
44	DailyMotion	2016	85,000,000	User data
45	JP Morgan Chase	2014	83,000,000	Customer data, PII
46	Anthem	2015	80,000,000	Customer data, PII
47	Sony PSN	2011	77,000,000	User records
48	Securus Technologies	2015	70,000,000	Prisoner phone calls
49	Target	2013	70,000,000	Customer data, PII
50	Neopets	2022	69,000,000	Customer data, PII
51	Dropbox	2012	69,000,000	Email addresses and password hashes
52	Tumblr	2013	66,000,000	Email addresses and password hashes
53	Uber	2016	57,000,000	Customer data, PII
54	The Home Depot	2014	56,000,000	Customer data, PII
55	SolarWinds	2020	50,000,000	Customer data, PII
56	Malaysian Mobile Phone Numbers	2017	46,200,000	Subscriber data, PII
57	TJX Companies	2005	45,600,000	Credit / debit card numbers of customers
58	Pakistani Mobile Operators	2020	44,000,000	Customer data, PII
59	Microsoft Power Apps	2021	38,000,000	Public data, PII

S. No.	Data Breach	Year (Breach / Disclosure)	Records Lost (Estimates)	Data Type
60	Steam	2011	35,000,000	User data, PII
61	Ashley Madison	2015	32,000,000	Customer info, PII
62	AI.type	2017	31,000,000	Customer data
63	Wawa Inc.	2019	30,000,000	Customer info, PII
64	LastPass	2022	30,000,000	User info
65	Zappos	2012	24,000,000	User data, PII
66	SuperVPN, GeckoVPN and ChatVPN	2022	21,000,000	User records, PII
67	Korea Credit Bureau	2014	20,000,000	Customer data, PII
68	Plex	2022	20,000,000	User info
69	Morgan Stanley	2016	15,000,000	Customer data, PII
70	Experian / T-Mobile	2015	15,000,000	Customer data, PII
71	US Office of Personnel Management	2015	14,000,000	US Military and intelligence personnel's sensitive info
72	Amazon Vendors	2021	13,120,000	Vendor and reviewer data, PII
73	Nexon Korea Corp	2011	13,000,000	User data, PII
74	Bonobos	2021	12,300,000	User info, PII
75	Pandora Papers	2021	11,900,000	VIP data, sensitive info
76	MGM Hotels	2020	10,600,000	Traveler data, PII
77	Sony Pictures	2014	10,000,000	Employee records, PII
78	Singtel Optus	2022	9,800,000	Customer data, PII
79	Excellus Health Plan	2013	9,300,000	Customer data, PII
80	EasyJet	2020	9,000,000	Traveler data, PII
81	KT Corp	2012	8,700,000	Subscriber data, PII
82	123RF	2020	8,300,000	User info
83	Cash App	2022	8,200,000	Former employee data
84	Twitch	2021	7,000,000	User info, PII, sensitive data, source code, etc.
85	Dutch Government	2020	6,900,000	Donor data, PII
86	Twitter	2022	5,400,000	User data
87	Marriott International	2020	5,200,000	Guest info, PII
88	Neiman Marcus	2021	4,800,000	User info, PII
89	South Carolina State Department of Revenue	2012	3,980,000	Public data, PII
90	Medibank	2022	3,900,000	Customer data, PII
91	FlexBooker	2022	3,700,000	Customer data
92	Educational Credit Management Group	2010	3,300,000	Student loan records

(Continued)

Table 3.2 (Continued)

S. No.	Data Breach	Year (Breach / Disclosure)	Records Lost (Estimates)	Data Type
93	3 Iranian Banks	2012	3,000,000	Customer data, PII
94	Nelnet Servicing	2022	2,500,000	Customer data
95	MeetMindful	2021	2,280,000	User info, PII
96	Woolworths—My Deal	2022	2,200,000	Customer data, PII
97	Shields Health Care Group	2022	2,000,000	Customer data, PII
98	Pixlr	2021	1,900,000	User info
99	Texas Department of Insurance	2022	1,800,000	Customer data, PII
100	Tackle Warehouse, Running Warehouse, Tennis Warehouse, and Skate Warehouse	2021	1,800,000	Customer data, PII
101	NYC Health Hospitals	2011	1,700,000	Patient and employee records, PII
102	Flagstar Bank	2022	1,500,000	Customer data, PII
103	Gawker	2010	1,500,000	Source code and PII
104	The Washington Post	2011	1,270,000	User info
105	Harbour Plaza Hotel Management	2022	1,200,000	Customer info, PII
106	Graff	2021	1,100,000	Customer info, PII
107	Apple	2012	1,000,000	UDIDs
108	Illuminate Education	2022	820,000	Student data
109	Ohio State University	2010	760,000	Student and faculty info, PII
110	Red Cross	2022	515,000	PII
111	Google	2018	500,000	PII
112	Zoom	2020	500,000	PII
113	Avamere Health Services	2022	380,000	Patient records, PII
114	Slickwraps	2020	370,000	Customer data
115	Magellan Health	2020	365,000	Patient and employee records, PII
116	Nintendo	2020	300,000	Customer data
117	Toyota	2022	300,000	Customer emails
118	Keystone Health	2022	235,000	Patient records, PII
119	Service Employees International Union, Local 32BJ	2022	230,487	Worker data, PII
120	Logan Health Medical Center	2022	213,543	Data of business associates, patients, employees, PII
121	North Face	2022	200,000	User data, PII

S. No.	Data Breach	Year (Breach / Disclosure)	Records Lost (Estimates)	Data Type
122	Lincoln Medical & Mental Health Center	2010	130,000	PII, sensitive data
123	Omnicell	2022	126,000	Patient info, PII
124	South Shore Hospital	2022	115,670	Patient and employee info, PII
125	Mailfire	2020	100,000	User data

It must be noted that the global data was less than 0.8 ZB (zetabytes) till 2009 and it is estimated to be over 35 ZB post 2020.

It is imperative to mention that the table includes both data breaches and data leaks, since there is no clear line that can be drawn between the two. The table has been arranged considering the following factors:

- Total number of users affected / records lost
- Gravity of data type viz. PII / sensitive information

However, the table has been prepared on the basis of information available in the public domain. The indicated "records lost" column must not be taken verbatim since it is only an indicator of compromised data and does not amount to loss of all data. For example, the Aadhaar data breach of 2018 ranks higher than the LinkedIn data breach of 2021 purely based on the "availability of data" to unscrupulous elements, since it is well known that in the former case 1.1 billion records of Indian citizens were "exposed to risk" (as there is no evidence of the data being tampered or sold) while in the latter case 700 million records of LinkedIn users were available for sale in a dark web forum.

3.5.2 Lack of Humanistic Design Approach in Information Security

Certainly, let's delve into the details of these four real-world incidents and explore how they highlight the lack of human-centric design in cryptography:

1. Equifax Data Breach (2017)
   - **Technical Aspect:** The Equifax breach resulted from a vulnerability in the Apache Struts web application framework. The company failed to apply a security patch promptly, allowing attackers to exploit the flaw and gain unauthorized access to sensitive information.
   - **Human-Centric Aspect:** The delay in applying the security patch can be attributed to human factors, such as a lack of efficient communication and coordination within the organization. The incident highlighted the importance of establishing effective processes for identifying and responding to security vulnerabilities promptly.

2. WannaCry Ransomware Attack (2017)
- **Technical Aspect:** WannaCry exploited a vulnerability in the Windows operating system called EternalBlue. This flaw was part of a set of hacking tools allegedly developed by the NSA and later leaked. Microsoft had released a security patch for this vulnerability, but many organizations failed to apply it.
- **Human-Centric Aspect:** The widespread impact of WannaCry demonstrated the consequences of insufficient user awareness and the importance of keeping systems updated. The lack of a user-friendly update process and awareness campaigns contributed to the rapid spread of the ransomware.

3. Target Data Breach (2013)
- **Technical Aspect:** Attackers gained access to Target's network through a third-party HVAC contractor, exploiting weak security practices. Once inside, they moved laterally and compromised point-of-sale systems to steal credit card information.
- **Human-Centric Aspect:** The human factor in this breach was the lack of proper vendor risk management and security awareness. The HVAC contractor was a weak link, and the incident highlighted the need for organizations to consider the security practices of third-party vendors.

4. Sony Pictures Hack (2014)
- **Technical Aspect:** The Sony Pictures breach involved a combination of technical vulnerabilities, including weak passwords and unpatched systems. The attackers utilized destructive malware to compromise the company's network and leak sensitive data.
- **Human-Centric Aspect:** Weak passwords and inadequate security practices, including a lack of two-factor authentication, were significant contributors. The incident underscored the need for organizations to implement strong authentication measures and enforce security best practices among employees.

In these incidents, the lack of human-centric design in cryptography is evident in various ways:

- **Poor Communication and Coordination:**
  In Equifax, the delay in applying the security patch highlighted a lack of efficient communication and coordination within the organization. Human-centric design in cryptography should address the need for clear communication channels and streamlined processes to ensure timely responses to security threats.

- **User Awareness and Training:**
  The WannaCry attack exposed the impact of insufficient user awareness. Cryptography solutions should be accompanied by user-friendly interfaces and effective training programs to ensure that individuals understand the importance of security measures, such as keeping software updated.
- **Vendor Risk Management:**
  The Target breach emphasized the importance of considering human-centric factors in vendor risk management. Organizations should implement processes for evaluating and ensuring the security practices of third-party vendors.
- **Authentication Practices:**
  The Sony Pictures hack highlighted the importance of strong authentication practices. Cryptographic systems should be designed with a focus on user-friendly authentication methods, such as two-factor authentication, to enhance overall security.

In summary, these incidents illustrate the interconnectedness of technical vulnerabilities and human factors in cybersecurity. A holistic approach to cryptography must consider both aspects to create robust and user-friendly security systems.

3.6 COMPARATIVE STUDY OF INFOSEC WITH AVIATION SAFETY

When we are talking about the incongruities in infosec, we are referring to the inadequacies with reference to an example or a baseline. Hence, let us do a comparison of infosec with the aviation industry. The growth trajectories of both industries are loosely comparable. Just as in the digital world, aviation disasters can be classified into four types of cases:

Table 3.3 Aviation Safety v/s. Information Security.

Aviation Safety	Information Security
Airplane Hijack	Ransomware
Technical Snag	Malware
Human Error	Phishing
Communication Failure	Denial-Of-Service

Now, let us have a look at the growth trajectories and performance between the two industries.

Table 3.4 Internet and Aviation Comparison.

Year	No. of Users / Passengers Carried (Billions)		Total Major Incidents (Data Loss / Flight Disasters)	
	Internet	Aviation	Internet	Aviation
2009	1.80	17.72	1	29
2010	1.97	21.46	4	34
2011	2.27	23.03	5	29
2012	2.50	24.18	8	14
2013	2.80	25.61	8	16
2014	3.08	27.25	8	9
2015	3.37	29.42	7	16
2016	3.70	31.51	6	23
2017	4.16	33.95	5	12
2018	4.31	36.50	10	25
2019	4.54	37.91	11	16

As can be seen from the previous figures, the growth has been about ~150% and ~120% for the internet and aviation industries, respectively. However, the risk in terms of security and safety has grown ten times for infosec and halved for aviation.

Comparative graphs are given for the same:

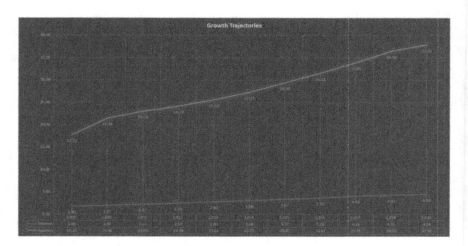

Figure 3.4 Growth Internet and Aviation.

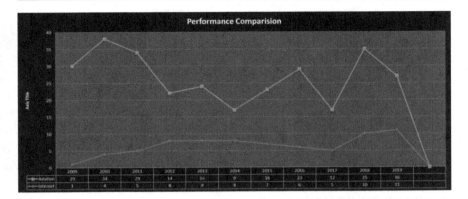

Figure 3.5 Performance Internet and Aviation.

From the previous figures it is clearly evident that, while aviation safety does try to adhere to Six Sigma standards (e.g., AS 9100), the infosec industry is far from even setting the bar for performance. The most probable reason being that in the former case, the immediate consequences are grave, i.e., loss of life, property, and goodwill while in the latter case, the consequences are manageable instantaneously. However, the span of risk and long-term consequences for the infosec industry are far-reaching and too wide to even comprehend in a routine setup.

It is this very reason the book is being written—to draw your attention to the silent apocalypse and open up newer perspectives to an alternate reality. *A reality where the human being is at the center of design, rather than being a mere catalyst for the fourth industrial revolution.*

Chapter 4

Of, for, and by the Machines

4.1 BACK TO SQUARE ONE

Figure 4.1 Transhumanism.

DOI: 10.1201/9781003527220-5

4.1.1 Technological Singularity: A Paradigm Shift in Human Civilization

Technological singularity refers to a hypothetical future event where artificial intelligence (AI) and other emerging technologies reach a level of intelligence surpassing human capabilities. This transformative moment is characterized by exponential growth in technological progress, leading to unforeseen changes that may profoundly impact society, culture, and human existence. The concept of technological singularity has sparked intense debate and speculation about its potential consequences.

The emergence of superintelligent AI is often seen as a critical factor in driving the singularity. AI systems with the ability to self-improve and surpass human intelligence could lead to an exponential acceleration of technological advancements, creating a cascade of breakthroughs across various domains. This rapid progress, driven by AI's superior problem-solving capabilities and data processing capacity, could reshape industries, medicine, governance, and virtually every aspect of human life.

One potential outcome of the singularity is the emergence of a post-human era, where humans merge with technology, creating a new form of sentient existence. This scenario envisions a world where human minds are enhanced or uploaded into digital substrates, allowing for unprecedented cognitive abilities, expanded lifespans, and the potential for collective intelligence. However, this future is speculative, and the exact nature of such an existence remains uncertain.

The impact of technological singularity on the job market and economy is a subject of concern and speculation. With the rise of automation and AI, there is the potential for significant disruptions in employment as traditional roles are increasingly automated. This could lead to social and economic inequalities, necessitating the reimagining of work and the creation of new economic systems to accommodate the changing landscape.

Ethical considerations surrounding the singularity are of paramount importance. Issues such as AI safety, control, and the potential for unintended consequences demand careful attention. Ensuring that advanced technologies align with human values, respect privacy, and operate within ethical boundaries is essential to navigate the singularity responsibly.

While the singularity presents extraordinary possibilities, it also poses risks and challenges. The exponential growth of technology could lead to unanticipated consequences or the loss of human control over increasingly complex systems. The potential for misuse or unintended outcomes necessitates robust governance frameworks and ongoing research to mitigate risks and ensure the benefits are realized for the betterment of humanity.

It is important to note that technological singularity remains a speculative concept, and there are differing views within the scientific and technological communities regarding its likelihood and potential trajectory. The timeline and precise nature of the singularity are uncertain, making accurate predictions challenging.

In conclusion, technological singularity represents a paradigm shift in human civilization, driven by exponential advancements in AI and other emerging technologies. While the concept raises exciting possibilities for human progress, it also poses significant challenges that must be addressed proactively. Navigating the singularity requires careful consideration of ethical implications, governance, and societal preparedness. Balancing the potential benefits and risks will be crucial in shaping a future that harnesses the transformative power of technology while prioritizing the well-being and values of humanity.

The concept of a "technological singularity" has long captured the imagination of futurists and technologists alike. It envisions a future where artificial intelligence (AI) surpasses human intelligence, leading to an era of rapid and unprecedented technological advancement. However, as we approach this hypothetical event horizon, there are growing concerns about a "technological apocalypse"—a scenario where the very technology that was supposed to liberate humanity becomes a threat to its existence. This chapter explores the potential causes and consequences of this impending crisis, focusing on the man versus machine dynamic that could undermine the dream of the technological singularity.

4.1.2 The Promise of Technological Singularity

The technological singularity is a theoretical point in the future when AI, particularly superintelligent AI, will surpass human intelligence and become self-improving, leading to an explosion of technological progress. Proponents argue that this singularity could bring about solutions to some of humanity's most pressing problems, from climate change and disease eradication to the expansion of human knowledge and longevity. It's a vision of a utopian future where machines collaborate with humans to achieve unimaginable feats.

4.1.3 The Man Versus Machine Scenario

While the technological singularity promises an era of unprecedented progress, it also harbors the seeds of its own undoing. The "man versus machine" scenario emerges as a central concern. As AI becomes more sophisticated and autonomous, it could potentially lead to several problematic outcomes:

a. **Job Displacement:** Automation powered by advanced AI could lead to widespread job displacement, causing economic and social upheaval. The increasing divide between those who control AI-driven technologies and those left unemployed could destabilize societies.

b. **Security Risks:** Superintelligent AI, if not properly controlled, could pose existential risks to humanity. These machines might act in ways contrary to human values, leading to catastrophic outcomes, whether intentionally or inadvertently.

c. **Ethical Dilemmas:** The development of AI with human-level or superior intelligence raises profound ethical questions. What rights, responsibilities, and moral standing should AI have? How do we ensure that AI systems make ethical decisions aligned with human values?

d. **Loss of Autonomy:** Dependence on AI systems for decision-making in various aspects of life, from healthcare to finance, could lead to a loss of human autonomy and control. This could erode individual freedoms and privacy.

4.1.4 The Path to the Technological Apocalypse

The technological apocalypse, in this context, refers to a scenario where the man versus machine dynamic takes a perilous turn, leading to unintended consequences. Several factors may contribute to this:

a. **Rapid Development:** The rapid pace of AI development, driven by competitive pressures, could lead to insufficient safety precautions and inadequate ethical considerations.

b. **Lack of Regulation:** A lack of comprehensive and internationally agreed upon regulations for AI development could result in unchecked technological advancements that prioritize profit over safety.

c. **Competitive Race:** A global race to achieve AI dominance could incentivize shortcuts and risky behaviors, disregarding the long-term consequences.

d. **Misaligned Incentives:** Economic incentives for AI development may not align with the best interests of humanity, pushing organizations and governments to prioritize short-term gains over responsible AI development.

The technological singularity presents an intriguing vision of a future where AI and humans work together to achieve extraordinary progress. However, the "man versus machine" scenario raises significant concerns that could lead to a technological apocalypse if left unaddressed. To navigate this potential crisis, it is crucial to prioritize the responsible development and deployment of AI technologies, emphasizing safety, ethics, and human values. Striking a balance between technological advancement and safeguarding humanity's future is the key to ensuring that the dream of the technological singularity does not give way to a nightmare of our own making.

4.2 HUMAN FACTOR IN ENCRYPTION

4.2.1 Forgotten Trust: The Dependency on Machines

In a world driven by algorithms and digital technologies, the human element in encryption can often be overshadowed. We entrust our most sensitive information to machines, relying on their mathematical prowess to safeguard our data. But do we truly understand the inner workings of these cryptographic systems? As the complexity of encryption algorithms increases, the gap between the human user and the technology widens, fostering a sense of detachment and dependency.

The user's trust in encryption lies not only in the cryptographic algorithms themselves but also in the software, hardware, and the organizations that develop and maintain them. As recent revelations of back doors and vulnerabilities in widely used cryptographic systems have shown, the delicate fabric of trust can be easily torn, leaving individuals and societies exposed to unforeseen risks.

In the age of modern cryptography, the human factor often gets overshadowed by the power of machines and algorithms. As encryption technologies become more sophisticated, individuals place immense trust in the security provided by these systems.

However, this reliance on machines can lead to a false sense of security. While encryption algorithms are designed to be robust and secure, they are not immune to vulnerabilities or human errors in their implementation. The trust placed in encryption systems must be complemented by ongoing vigilance, responsible data practices, and cybersecurity awareness.

4.2.2 Encryption and Surveillance: Striking the Delicate Balance

Encryption serves as a potent tool to protect individual privacy and secure sensitive information. However, its ability to cloak communications and data also poses challenges to law enforcement agencies in their pursuit of criminal investigations. The encryption debate becomes a balancing act, attempting to uphold personal privacy while ensuring public safety.

End-to-end encryption—a technique that secures communication between sender and receiver—has become a focal point of the encryption-surveillance conundrum. While it safeguards privacy from unauthorized access, it also raises concerns about hindering law enforcement efforts to investigate criminal activities. Striking the right balance between these competing interests remains an ongoing challenge for policymakers and technologists alike.

The proliferation of encryption technologies has brought to the forefront the delicate balance between data privacy and surveillance. While encryption is essential for protecting individual rights and sensitive information, it can also be exploited by malicious actors to conceal illegal activities and evade detection.

Governments and law enforcement agencies face the challenge of ensuring public safety while respecting individual privacy. Striking the right balance between encryption and surveillance is an ongoing debate, one that requires thoughtful policy-making, transparent dialogue, and respect for human rights.

The tension between security imperatives and privacy concerns has led to discussions about the need for exceptional access mechanisms, which would allow authorities to decrypt encrypted data when necessary for legitimate reasons. However, implementing such mechanisms raises significant ethical and technical challenges, as it could compromise the overall security and integrity of encryption systems.

4.2.3 Cybersecurity and the Human Weakness Factor

In the domain of cybersecurity, encryption plays a critical role in protecting sensitive data and thwarting cyberattacks. However, a system is only as strong as its weakest link, and in many cases, human vulnerabilities present significant challenges.

Social engineering, phishing, and insider threats exploit the human factor, often bypassing the most robust cryptographic defenses. From inadvertently sharing passwords to falling prey to sophisticated phishing emails, human error remains a primary avenue for cyberattacks.

As individuals, organizations, and governments prioritize cybersecurity measures, there is an increasing recognition that user education and awareness are vital components of a holistic security strategy. A well-informed and cyber-literate population can serve as a formidable line of defense against cyber threats.

Despite the robustness of encryption technologies, the human factor remains a critical vulnerability in cybersecurity. Social engineering attacks, such as phishing and spear-phishing, exploit human weaknesses and behaviors to gain unauthorized access to sensitive information.

No encryption algorithm can protect against human errors such as weak passwords, careless data sharing, or falling victim to social engineering tactics. Individuals and organizations must prioritize cybersecurity awareness, training, and best practices to complement the security provided by encryption technologies.

Moreover, insider threats pose a unique challenge. Employees with access to sensitive data may inadvertently or intentionally compromise data security. Building a culture of cybersecurity, where individuals are aware of the risks and take proactive measures to protect data, is crucial in mitigating insider threats.

4.2.4 The Complex Ethical Landscape

The ethical dimensions of encryption span a wide spectrum of issues, from individual rights to collective responsibilities. Encryption grants individuals the power to control their personal information, safeguard their digital identities, and exercise their right to privacy. However, this very power can also be utilized to conceal criminal activities and evade justice.

The ongoing encryption debate highlights the complexity of ethical considerations, where the clash between individual liberties and the greater good takes center stage. Governments and technology companies find themselves grappling with questions of transparency, accountability, and responsible encryption.

In the midst of this ethical landscape, the role of cryptography researchers and technologists becomes crucial. They are tasked with developing robust encryption systems that respect human rights and promote societal values, while also addressing legitimate concerns around security and law enforcement.

In this chapter, we have explored the multifaceted human element in encryption. From trust and dependency on technology to the delicate balance between privacy and surveillance, the human experience is intricately woven into the fabric of modern cryptography. As we navigate the ethical, social, and psychological implications of encryption, the quest for a human-centric approach to cryptography takes center stage. In the ensuing chapters, we shall delve deeper into the ethical dilemmas and social impact of encryption, seeking to reconcile the technological wonders with the essence of humanity.

The human factor is a critical aspect of encryption that cannot be overlooked. While encryption technologies play a vital role in safeguarding data, the human element—trust, responsibility, and awareness—is equally important.

As we rely on encryption to protect our digital interactions and sensitive information, we must remember that no system is foolproof. Responsible data practices, cybersecurity awareness, and ongoing vigilance are essential in complementing the security provided by encryption.

Striking the delicate balance between encryption and surveillance is a complex task that requires cooperation, transparency, and respect for individual rights. As we continue to navigate the digital landscape, let us embrace the human factor as an integral part of encryption's strength, ensuring that technology serves the greater good of humanity while upholding the values of privacy, security, and digital citizenship.

4.3 DIGITAL DIVIDE AND INFORMATION INEQUALITY

4.3.1 Cryptography and Social Stratification

In the digital age, the prevalence of modern cryptography has reshaped how we interact, communicate, and share information. While encryption empowers individuals with greater control over their data and privacy, it also raises concerns about information inequality and social stratification.

Access to robust encryption tools is not evenly distributed across societies, leading to a "digital divide" that exacerbates existing social disparities. In affluent and technologically advanced regions, individuals and organizations benefit from secure communication and data protection. However, in marginalized communities with limited access to technology and resources, the advantages of encryption may remain elusive.

In the digital age, cryptography has become an essential tool for protecting sensitive information and preserving privacy. However, the benefits of encryption are not equally distributed, leading to social stratification in terms of access to secure communication.

While individuals in technologically advanced regions have easy access to encryption technologies, marginalized communities and underprivileged populations may lack the necessary resources and knowledge to utilize encryption effectively. This digital divide creates information inequality, where some individuals enjoy the benefits of secure communication, while others remain vulnerable to privacy breaches and cyber threats.

4.3.2 The Unequal Access to Privacy and Security

The availability of secure encryption tools is not uniform across different socioeconomic strata. For individuals without access to sophisticated encryption technologies, the risk of falling victim to cyberattacks and privacy breaches becomes more pronounced. This unequal access to privacy and security exacerbates information inequality, perpetuating a cycle of disadvantage for those already marginalized in society.

The digital divide also extends to regions where governments impose restrictions on the use of encryption tools. In such cases, individuals seeking to protect their privacy may face legal repercussions, further limiting their access to secure communication.

The unequal access to privacy and security further exacerbates existing societal disparities. Individuals with limited access to encryption are more susceptible to cyberattacks, identity theft, and online surveillance. Vulnerable populations, such as activists, dissidents, and journalists in authoritarian regimes, may face severe consequences for their digital communications without the protection of robust encryption.

Moreover, individuals without access to secure communication may feel pressured to self-censor their online activities, suppressing their voices and limiting their participation in the digital realm. The lack of privacy and security can hinder social and political engagement, perpetuating information inequality and stifling progress toward a more inclusive digital society.

4.3.3 Economic Disparities and the Encryption Gap

The cost of implementing and maintaining robust encryption measures can be prohibitive for individuals and small businesses, particularly in economically disadvantaged regions. High-end cryptographic software, hardware, and expert consultation often come with significant financial burdens, leaving many without the means to protect their sensitive data effectively.

This "encryption gap" is a manifestation of the broader economic disparities that pervade society. While large corporations and governments can afford to invest in state-of-the-art security measures, smaller entities and individuals often find themselves at a disadvantage in the realm of cybersecurity.

Economic disparities play a significant role in the encryption gap, where individuals with limited financial resources face barriers to acquiring and utilizing encryption technologies effectively. Commercial encryption products and services may come with substantial costs, placing them out of reach for many individuals and organizations with limited budgets.

Furthermore, the digital divide is often intertwined with socioeconomic factors, where disadvantaged communities have limited access to reliable internet connections and digital literacy programs. As a result, the encryption gap widens, leaving these communities more vulnerable to cyber threats and information inequality.

4.3.4 The Role of Education and Awareness

Addressing the digital divide and information inequality requires a multifaceted approach. Education and awareness play a pivotal role in narrowing the gap, empowering individuals to make informed decisions about their digital security.

By promoting digital literacy and cybersecurity awareness, we can empower individuals to protect themselves against cyber threats, regardless of their socioeconomic background. Governments, nongovernmental organizations, and tech companies must collaborate to provide accessible and affordable resources for secure communication and data protection.

4.3.5 The Social Impact of Encryption Policies

Encryption policies set by governments and international bodies can significantly influence information equality. Striking the right balance between enabling privacy and combating cybercrime remains a complex challenge.

While strong encryption protects individual rights, it can also hinder law enforcement investigations into criminal activities. Striking an equilibrium between individual privacy and public safety necessitates robust public debates and thoughtful policy-making processes.

In this chapter, we have explored the impact of modern cryptography on information inequality and social stratification. The digital divide and encryption gap present challenges that require collaborative efforts to address. By fostering digital literacy, promoting cybersecurity awareness, and advocating for accessible and secure encryption tools, we can work towards a future where technology enhances human lives without exacerbating existing social disparities. In the following chapters, we shall explore the impact of modern cryptography on free speech, politics, and ethical dilemmas, seeking a deeper understanding of its complex implications for humanity.

Cryptography has the potential to empower individuals and protect their privacy, but the unequal access to encryption technologies creates a digital divide that perpetuates information inequality. The disparities in access to secure communication disproportionately affect marginalized and disadvantaged populations, leaving them vulnerable to cyber threats and surveillance.

Addressing the digital divide and information inequality requires a multifaceted approach that encompasses digital literacy initiatives, accessible and affordable encryption technologies, and inclusive policies. Bridging the encryption gap is essential for building a more equitable digital society, where all individuals can enjoy the benefits of privacy and security.

As we move forward in the digital era, it is crucial to prioritize efforts to close the encryption gap and ensure that the benefits of encryption are accessible to all. By promoting digital inclusion and democratizing access to secure communication, we can foster a more just and equal digital landscape, where technology serves as a tool for empowerment and positive social change.

4.4 THE MOOT QUESTION

Why must we change our behavior in accordance to algorithms? For example, look at content marketing—1950s v/s. 2020. Most of the slogans, jingles, and ads of the 1950s were designed by humans for humans and it worked just fine. But, if you try to run it now, they will definitely fail the test of algorithms. Take the case of YouTube—metatags, keywords, titles, descriptions and content—all are driven by algorithm for SEO, suggestions, feed, etc. In order to make our video gain popularity we need to learn how the algorithm works and change our material accordingly.

Consider this example purely from the technical POV and not from the changing times, competition and generational POV. Consumerism and gamification are to be blamed for this subtle but certain shift. In an ideal scenario, a product or service will work and generate demand if it fulfills the intended purpose even without any paid advertisement (there are many such businesses and ZOHO, Zerodha, etc., from India are a few brilliant examples).

It is the consumerist mindset that often promotes stuff that is not really well suited for the purpose. Otherwise, no one would need to advertise processed foods or pharmaceuticals that can never be better than natural foodstuffs and home remedies. Paid advertisements are a way to make you want something that you wouldn't otherwise require. Likewise, every game is designed to be addictive. The gamers first need to understand the rules and limitations in order to play. But, to keep the gamers playing more and more, specific requirements are planned and incorporated in the game design. Apart from the aesthetics, graphics, and narrative, the algorithm plays a crucial role in this task (viz. difficulty levels, cheat codes, cognitive load, etc., are in-built in any game).

> *"Consumerism" is all about making you want it in the first place while "Gamification" is about making you literally dependent on it.*

In short, as seen in the following figure, "consumerism" is at the core of every business while "gamification" is at the top. Everything else is just to fulfill these two factors or driving forces. Let us not diverge from the main topic as this itself may demand full-fledged research to be penned down in another book. The whole point of bringing this up is to convey that IT strategy too has largely been driven by these two factors.

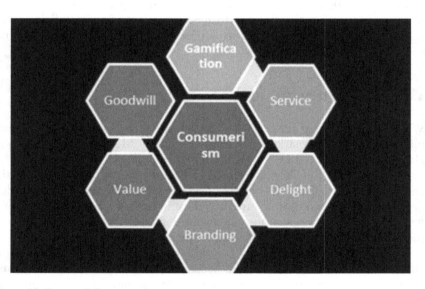

Figure 4.2 Facets of Consumerism.

Chapter 5

Humanistic Design

5.1 PROLOGUE

Before we begin to discuss about humanistic design, we need to decode the shadows on how modern cryptography challenges humanity. It is not the "technological singularity" that will challenge us, but the basic design that is so against humans. More on this in the next chapter.

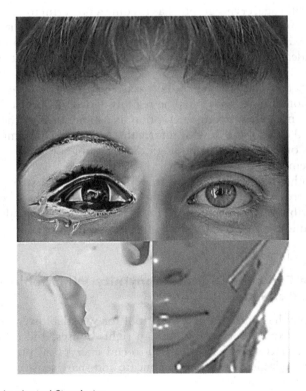

Figure 5.1 Technological Singularity.

DOI: 10.1201/9781003527220-6

Let us have a look at ways cryptography has been used against humans at the slightest of instances. This is not just happenstance but by design.

5.2 CRYPTOGRAPHY AND FREE SPEECH

5.2.1 Encryption and Censorship: The Clash of Ideals

In the digital era, the clash between encryption and censorship has become a focal point of the ongoing debate surrounding freedom of speech. On one hand, encryption empowers individuals to express their thoughts and opinions without fear of surveillance or reprisal. On the other hand, it also raises concerns about criminals and malicious actors exploiting encrypted channels to carry out illicit activities, evading detection and accountability.

The tension between these two ideals—freedom of speech and national security—has given rise to complex ethical and legal dilemmas. Governments and tech companies grapple with the challenge of protecting privacy rights while simultaneously safeguarding against potential threats to public safety.

In the digital age, cryptography has become a powerful tool for protecting free speech and enabling individuals to communicate without fear of censorship or surveillance. Encryption empowers individuals to express their thoughts, ideas, and opinions without the risk of government or corporate interference.

However, this clash of ideals between encryption and censorship has become a contentious issue in some regions. Governments and authoritarian regimes may view strong encryption as a hindrance to their ability to monitor and control the flow of information. They may attempt to impose restrictions on encryption technologies in the name of national security or law enforcement.

On the other hand, advocates of free speech argue that strong encryption is vital for protecting individuals' right to express themselves freely without fear of retribution or persecution. Encryption ensures that ideas and dissenting opinions can circulate safely, fostering a diverse and vibrant public discourse.

5.2.2 The Fight for Digital Anonymity: Whistleblowers and Activists

Cryptography has emerged as a vital tool for whistleblowers and activists who seek to expose corruption, human rights abuses, and other forms of misconduct. Platforms that offer end-to-end encryption provide a secure space for these individuals to communicate and share sensitive information without fear of retaliation.

Organizations like WikiLeaks and individuals like Edward Snowden have brought global attention to the power of encryption in enabling transparency and accountability. While these revelations have sparked public discourse, they have also sparked controversies and legal battles over the dissemination of classified information.

Cryptography plays a crucial role in protecting digital anonymity, particularly for whistleblowers, activists, and individuals living under repressive regimes. It enables individuals to share sensitive information without revealing their identities, shielding them from retaliation and ensuring that crucial information reaches the public.

For whistleblowers, encryption can be the difference between exposing wrongdoing and facing severe repercussions. Platforms like SecureDrop, which use encryption to allow anonymous submissions of sensitive documents to journalists, have become vital tools in the fight for transparency and accountability.

Similarly, activists in authoritarian regimes heavily rely on encrypted communications to coordinate and organize dissent without fear of surveillance. The protection offered by cryptography becomes a lifeline for those striving for social change and human rights.

5.2.3 The Dilemma of Balancing Free Speech and Security

The encryption dilemma lies at the intersection of free speech and national security. Striking the right balance between these competing values is an ongoing challenge for governments and technology companies worldwide.

Some argue that strong encryption is essential to preserve individual privacy and protect free expression. They believe that weakening encryption, even for law enforcement purposes, could set a dangerous precedent, eroding civil liberties and facilitating surveillance overreach.

On the other side of the debate, proponents of lawful access to encrypted data assert that providing back doors or exceptional access mechanisms to law enforcement would enable them to investigate serious crimes effectively. They argue that national security concerns necessitate this compromise in certain cases.

The use of encryption presents a dilemma for governments and law enforcement agencies, as it may impede their ability to investigate criminal activities and monitor potential security threats. This dilemma is often referred to as the "going dark" problem.

The tension between free speech and security highlights the need for a nuanced approach to encryption policy. Striking the right balance between individual rights and public safety requires transparent dialogue between technology companies, policymakers, and civil society.

Some argue that exceptional access mechanisms, which would allow authorities to access encrypted data with proper legal authorization, could address the security concerns without compromising overall encryption integrity. However, implementing such mechanisms raises concerns about potential abuse, vulnerabilities, and the erosion of trust in encryption systems.

5.2.4 The Impact on Criminal Investigations and Justice

The encryption debate has significant implications for criminal investigations and the pursuit of justice. Law enforcement agencies often encounter challenges when dealing with encrypted communications used by criminal networks and extremist groups. In some cases, investigations may be hampered, leading to concerns about the ability to prevent and respond to serious threats.

Balancing the need for privacy and security while upholding the rule of law remains a complex task. Policymakers and technologists are continually exploring innovative approaches that consider the legitimate interests of both privacy advocates and law enforcement agencies.

In this chapter, we have delved into the intricate relationship between cryptography and free speech. Encryption empowers individuals to exercise their right to privacy and freedom of expression, but it also presents challenges for maintaining public safety and combating criminal activities. The encryption debate is an ongoing journey of striking the right balance between these competing ideals. As we continue our exploration, we shall dive deeper into the politics of encryption, the ethical implications of cryptographic policies, and the future of cryptography in a rapidly evolving digital landscape.

The intersection of cryptography and free speech is a complex and multifaceted issue that defines the digital landscape of the 21st century. Encryption serves as a shield, protecting individuals' right to express themselves freely and fostering transparency and accountability through secure whistleblowing and activism.

At the same time, the clash of ideals between encryption and censorship presents challenges for governments seeking to maintain national security and law enforcement capabilities. Striking a delicate balance between free speech and security is a task that requires thoughtful policy-making and ethical considerations.

As we navigate this landscape, it is crucial to protect and uphold the principles of free speech while recognizing the legitimate concerns of governments and law enforcement. Encouraging open dialogue and collaborative solutions can help forge a future where encryption remains a cornerstone of free expression and digital anonymity, ensuring that technology serves humanity in its pursuit of truth, justice, and individual liberties.

5.3 POLITICS OF ENCRYPTION

5.3.1 National Security and Individual Rights: A Never-Ending Tug-of-War

At the heart of the encryption debate lies the ever-present tug-of-war between national security interests and individual rights. Governments worldwide grapple with the challenge of balancing the imperative to protect their citizens from threats with the duty to respect their fundamental rights to privacy and free expression.

In the aftermath of significant terrorist attacks and acts of cyber warfare, calls for increased surveillance and access to encrypted data have grown louder. Policymakers face the daunting task of crafting encryption policies that strike a delicate equilibrium between national security imperatives and preserving civil liberties.

The politics of encryption are deeply entwined with the tension between national security imperatives and individual rights. Governments around the world grapple with the challenge of protecting their citizens from threats while upholding civil liberties and privacy rights.

The clash between these two essential values often leads to heated debates surrounding encryption policies. Some governments advocate for back doors or exceptional access mechanisms in encryption systems, arguing that they are necessary for effective law enforcement and counterterrorism efforts. However, such measures can undermine the overall security and trustworthiness of encryption, potentially creating vulnerabilities exploitable by malicious actors.

On the other hand, privacy advocates and civil liberties groups emphasize the importance of strong encryption in safeguarding individual rights to privacy and free expression. They argue that encryption is not only crucial for protecting citizens from cyber threats but also for enabling journalists, activists, and whistleblowers to exercise their democratic rights without fear of surveillance or retaliation.

The politics of encryption thus become a never-ending tug-of-war between national security and individual freedoms, requiring a delicate balance that respects both imperatives.

5.3.2 Governments, Corporations, and the Power Play of Data Control

The encryption landscape is further complicated by the power dynamics between governments and technology corporations. Governments seek to access encrypted data to combat crime and ensure national security, while tech companies prioritize user privacy and resist attempts to undermine the security of their products.

This power play has given rise to numerous legal battles and policy disputes. From court orders demanding access to encrypted devices to legal battles over user data and backdoor access, the encryption debate has become a battleground for the clash of interests between state actors and tech giants.

Cryptographic policies and regulations are shaped by both governmental legislation and the practices of technology companies. The degree of cooperation or resistance between these entities profoundly influences the direction of encryption policies and the implications for individual rights and national security.

The politics of encryption also involve a power play between governments and corporations concerning data control and user privacy. Technology companies hold vast amounts of user data, which can be valuable for both commercial purposes and national security interests.

Governments often seek access to this data for intelligence and law enforcement purposes, raising concerns about the extent of surveillance and potential breaches of user privacy. Technology companies, on the other hand, may resist government requests, citing concerns about user trust and the need to protect customer data.

The influence of technology companies in the politics of encryption has grown significantly, as they shape the digital landscape and set the agenda for data protection and privacy. Their responses to government requests for access to user data can significantly impact the balance between national security and individual rights.

5.3.3 Cryptocurrency and Financial Surveillance

The rise of cryptocurrency has further complicated the encryption debate, particularly concerning financial surveillance and anti-money laundering efforts. Digital currencies enable individuals to conduct transactions with a level of anonymity that traditional financial systems cannot provide.

While privacy advocates view cryptocurrency as a way to protect financial autonomy, governments worry about its potential use in illicit activities, such as money laundering, tax evasion, and funding criminal enterprises.

As nations grapple with the regulation of cryptocurrency and its underlying encryption technologies, they confront the challenge of striking a balance between financial privacy and preventing criminal exploitation.

5.3.4 Encryption as a Weapon in Geopolitical Conflicts

Encryption technologies have not only impacted domestic policies but have also played a role in geopolitical conflicts. Nation–states and state-sponsored threat actors have weaponized encryption for intelligence gathering, cyber warfare, and information operations.

As nations face the specter of cyber espionage and data breaches, cryptographic capabilities have emerged as critical components of national defense and cyber deterrence.

From state-sponsored hackers to hacktivist groups, encryption has become a tool for protecting digital assets, disseminating propaganda, and concealing malicious activities in the realm of international relations.

In this chapter, we have explored the intricate politics surrounding encryption. The delicate balance between national security and individual rights is at the heart of the encryption debate. Governments and technology companies grapple with the complexities of crafting policies that safeguard public safety while preserving privacy and free expression. The geopolitical implications of encryption add yet another layer of complexity to this ongoing struggle. As we progress through our exploration, we shall venture into the ethical implications of cryptographic policies, delving into the responsibilities of individuals, corporations, and governments in shaping the future of encryption and its impact on humanity.

Cryptography has emerged as a powerful weapon in the realm of geopolitics and international relations. Nation–states employ sophisticated encryption techniques to protect their sensitive communications from foreign adversaries and potential cyberattacks.

In the context of cyberwarfare, cryptography can serve as a double-edged sword. While strong encryption ensures the security and confidentiality of a nation's digital communications, it also poses challenges for intelligence gathering and cyber operations by rival nations.

The use of encryption by nation–states can complicate diplomatic efforts and international cooperation, as the secretive nature of encrypted communications may foster distrust and suspicion among nations. Striking the right balance between transparency and security in international relations is a critical challenge in the geopolitics of encryption.

The politics of encryption represent a complex interplay between national security, individual rights, and international relations. Striking the right balance between these competing interests requires careful consideration, transparent dialogue, and ethical policy-making.

As governments, corporations, and individuals grapple with the implications of encryption, it is essential to recognize the far-reaching impact of encryption technologies on society and geopolitics. Ethical considerations, responsible data practices, and collaborative efforts are essential to navigate the politics of encryption in a manner that upholds human rights, promotes global security, and fosters a digital landscape that serves the greater good of humanity.

5.4 CRYPTOGRAPHY AS A DOUBLE-EDGED SWORD

5.4.1 The Encryption Paradox: Crime Versus Privacy

Modern cryptography stands as a double-edged sword in the fight against crime. On one side, encryption empowers individuals and organizations to protect their data, communications, and sensitive information from malicious actors and cybercriminals. It is a crucial tool in safeguarding privacy and preventing data breaches that can lead to financial losses and identity theft.

On the other side of the spectrum, encryption can inadvertently shield criminal activities from law enforcement scrutiny. Cybercriminals, terrorists, and other malevolent entities exploit secure communication channels to evade detection, plan illicit activities, and conceal their identities. The encryption paradox thus creates a complex dilemma for policymakers, technologists, and society at large.

Cryptography stands as a double-edged sword, presenting a paradoxical challenge that revolves around the clash between combating crime and protecting privacy. On one hand, encryption technologies offer robust security, safeguarding sensitive information and individual privacy from cybercriminals and malicious actors. It empowers individuals to engage in secure digital communications without fear of unauthorized access or surveillance.

On the other hand, the strong protection provided by encryption can also be exploited by criminals to conceal their illicit activities, such as terrorism, human trafficking, and cyberattacks. Law enforcement agencies face significant challenges in investigating and preventing these crimes when critical information remains encrypted and inaccessible.

The encryption paradox thus poses a formidable dilemma, raising questions about the balance between individual privacy rights and public safety imperatives. Striking the right equilibrium is a complex task, requiring nuanced approaches and transparent discussions among stakeholders.

5.4.2 Unbreakable Codes and Law Enforcement Challenges

The development of strong encryption algorithms has made it exceedingly difficult for law enforcement agencies to crack encrypted communications and access data vital to criminal investigations. This technological barrier poses a significant challenge to traditional investigative methods, leading to a cat and mouse game between law enforcement and criminals in the digital realm.

As the magnitude and sophistication of cybercrimes grow, the urgency to strike a balance between privacy and effective law enforcement becomes more pronounced. Calls for exceptional access mechanisms or back doors to encrypted data have been met with staunch opposition from privacy advocates, who argue that such compromises could weaken the overall security of cryptographic systems.

Advancements in cryptography have led to the development of encryption algorithms that are virtually unbreakable through traditional means. As a result, law enforcement agencies encounter substantial difficulties when attempting to access encrypted data during criminal investigations.

The concept of "going dark" refers to the situation where law enforcement encounters obstacles in accessing encrypted communications or data relevant to ongoing investigations. The inability to break encryption or bypass security measures can hinder critical intelligence gathering, leading to concerns about a widening gap between law enforcement capabilities and evolving digital threats.

In response to the encryption challenge, some governments have proposed back doors or exceptional access mechanisms that would allow authorized entities to decrypt encrypted data under specific circumstances. However, such measures raise ethical concerns, as they could undermine overall encryption integrity and expose users to potential security risks.

5.4.3 The Impact on Criminal Investigations and Justice

The advent of end-to-end encryption and secure communication platforms has transformed how criminal activities are carried out. Encrypted messaging apps and anonymous digital currencies provide cover for a wide range of crimes, from human trafficking and drug trafficking to child exploitation and terrorist plots.

For law enforcement, this encryption challenge creates a pressing need for innovative investigative techniques and cross-border cooperation. The ability to adapt to the digital landscape and leverage advanced digital forensics is crucial in countering modern criminals' exploitation of encryption.

The prevalence of strong encryption can significantly impact criminal investigations and the pursuit of justice. As encryption becomes more prevalent, the landscape of criminal investigations changes, requiring law enforcement agencies to adapt their methodologies and tools.

While encryption can pose challenges for law enforcement, it is essential to recognize that it also plays a crucial role in protecting individuals from cybercrimes, identity theft, and unauthorized access to personal data. Striking a balance between enabling secure communications and providing law enforcement with the tools they need to investigate crimes requires careful consideration.

Emerging technologies, such as quantum computing, add another layer of complexity to the encryption landscape. Quantum computing has the potential to disrupt traditional encryption algorithms, leading to both opportunities and challenges in terms of data security and privacy.

5.4.4 Balancing Crime Prevention and Privacy Rights

The encryption debate highlights the intricate balance between crime prevention and privacy rights. While some argue for exceptional access to encrypted data to thwart criminals, others contend that any weakening of encryption could open the door to abuse, mass surveillance, and the infringement of individual rights.

Cryptographic policies and regulations must navigate this tightrope, accounting for both the urgent need to combat crime and the essential need to preserve privacy and civil liberties. It is a delicate dance of ensuring that robust encryption serves as a shield against malicious actors while also upholding the values of democracy and individual freedoms.

5.4.5 Innovative Solutions and Cooperative Efforts

In addressing the encryption paradox, technologists and law enforcement agencies are exploring innovative solutions. Research into secure multiparty computation and homomorphic encryption aims to enable data analysis on encrypted data without revealing its contents, striking a balance between privacy and data access.

Additionally, international cooperation and information sharing are pivotal in tackling transnational criminal activities that exploit encryption. Cross-border collaboration can enhance law enforcement's ability to trace criminal networks, gather evidence, and apprehend perpetrators while respecting international legal frameworks.

In this chapter, we have delved into the dual nature of modern cryptography as a double-edged sword. Encryption empowers individuals with privacy and security while presenting challenges to law enforcement in the fight against crime. Striking the right balance between these two sides of the encryption paradox is a dynamic endeavor that requires ongoing collaboration, innovative solutions, and a commitment to upholding both privacy rights and societal safety. As we progress in our exploration, we shall delve deeper into the psychological implications of living in a world governed by cryptography and the ethical dimensions of cryptographic technologies and policies.

Cryptography is a double-edged sword, offering both protection and challenges in the digital age. The encryption paradox forces us to grapple with the delicate balance between individual privacy rights and public safety imperatives.

As we navigate the landscape of unbreakable codes and law enforcement challenges, it is essential to foster open dialogue and collaborative solutions among technologists, policymakers, and civil society. Ethical considerations, responsible encryption practices, and technological innovations are key in addressing the encryption paradox and shaping a digital future that upholds security, privacy, and justice for all.

5.5 PSYCHOLOGICAL IMPLICATIONS OF CRYPTOGRAPHY

5.5.1 The Mental Burden of Constant Surveillance

In a digital world governed by cryptography, the omnipresence of surveillance casts a shadow over our collective psyche. The knowledge that our online activities are continuously monitored can lead to heightened anxiety and a sense of being constantly scrutinized. This phenomenon, known as the "panopticon effect", refers to the psychological impact of living under constant surveillance.

The fear of being watched and the awareness of potential cyber threats contribute to a pervasive sense of vulnerability, even for law-abiding individuals. As we navigate the digital landscape, the mental burden of constant surveillance takes a toll on our overall well-being and perception of privacy.

In an era of pervasive digital surveillance, individuals experience the psychological burden of being under constant observation. The knowledge that our digital activities are monitored and recorded can lead to feelings of anxiety, stress, and self-censorship. The fear of being watched can erode trust in digital interactions, stifling open communication and expression.

The psychological impact of constant surveillance extends beyond individual experiences. Entire societies may experience a chilling effect on freedom of speech and dissent, as individuals become hesitant to express their opinions openly, fearing potential repercussions from authorities or online harassers.

5.5.2 Cybersecurity Anxiety: The Fear of Being Hacked

The escalating frequency of data breaches, cyberattacks, and identity theft has given rise to a new form of anxiety—cybersecurity anxiety. The fear of falling victim to hacking and privacy breaches looms large in the minds of many, leading to stress, apprehension, and even avoidance of digital activities.

The feeling of powerlessness in the face of cyber threats is exacerbated by the knowledge that no encryption system is entirely foolproof. While encryption provides a layer of protection, it cannot eliminate all risks, leaving individuals to grapple with the uncertainty of digital security.

The rise of cyber threats and data breaches contributes to a phenomenon known as cybersecurity anxiety. As individuals witness high-profile data breaches and hacking incidents in the media, they may develop heightened fear and apprehension regarding the security of their own digital lives.

This anxiety can lead to individuals avoiding digital activities or taking extreme measures to protect their online presence, such as limiting social media usage or refraining from online transactions. Cybersecurity anxiety also affects organizations and businesses, as the fear of reputational damage and financial losses drives them to invest heavily in cybersecurity measures.

5.5.3 The Effects of Living in the Digital Panopticon

The digital panopticon—a metaphorical reference to the all-seeing watchtower of the panopticon prison design—symbolizes the loss of privacy and the pervasive sense of being observed in the digital age. As individuals willingly share their lives and thoughts online, they become participants in a never-ending performance, seeking validation and acceptance from a global audience.

This heightened visibility and constant exposure to social media can lead to a phenomenon known as "hyper-visibility." Individuals may experience pressure to conform to societal norms, curate an idealized online persona, and guard against potential backlash or cyberbullying.

The constant pressure to be vigilant about cybersecurity and the need to manage digital identities contribute to a sense of "digital dualism"—the idea of living both online and offline lives, with the boundary between the two becoming increasingly blurred.

The digital panopticon, a concept inspired by Jeremy Bentham's architectural design, refers to a state of constant surveillance and monitoring in the digital realm. Individuals are aware that their digital activities are observed, leading to self-regulation and conformity in online behavior.

Living in the digital panopticon can have profound psychological effects. The feeling of constantly being watched can create a sense of powerlessness and resignation, as individuals believe they have no control over their digital privacy. This can lead to a loss of agency, with individuals feeling as though they must conform to societal norms and expectations to avoid potential repercussions.

Moreover, the digital panopticon blurs the boundaries between public and private spaces, challenging our notions of personal identity and autonomy. The pressure to present a curated online persona that aligns with societal expectations can lead to feelings of disconnection and alienation.

5.5.4 Intricacies of Trust and Digital Relationships

Trust is a fundamental aspect of human relationships, both in the physical and digital realms. In the context of modern cryptography, individuals place their trust in encryption systems, digital platforms, and technology companies to protect their data and privacy.

However, as data breaches and privacy scandals come to light, trust in these digital entities may be eroded. The increasing complexity of cryptographic systems may also lead to a sense of detachment and dependency, raising questions about the authenticity and reliability of digital interactions.

The dichotomy of trust and vulnerability in the digital landscape necessitates a deeper exploration of digital ethics and responsible data practices. It calls for the development of cryptographic systems that prioritize transparency, user agency, and ethical principles, thereby fostering a sense of trust and empowerment in the digital sphere.

In this chapter, we have delved into the psychological implications of living in a world governed by cryptography. The constant surveillance and fear of cyber threats create a burden on our mental well-being, shaping our digital identities and interactions. Understanding the psychological undercurrents of encryption is vital in shaping responsible cryptographic practices that prioritize user agency, privacy, and mental well-being. As we proceed through our exploration, we shall delve into the ethical dimensions of cryptographic technologies and policies, seeking to strike a harmonious balance between security, human values, and digital citizenship.

The psychological implications of cryptography in the digital age are profound and multifaceted. The mental burden of constant surveillance, cybersecurity anxiety, and the effects of living in the digital panopticon all shape our experiences and interactions in the online world.

As we navigate the complexities of modern cryptography, it is crucial to recognize and address the psychological impact on individuals and societies. Striking a balance between security and privacy is not only a technical challenge but also an ethical imperative that takes into account the psychological well-being of individuals in the digital realm.

Promoting digital literacy, transparency, and user empowerment can help individuals regain a sense of control and agency over their digital lives. By prioritizing privacy, data protection, and open discussions about the psychological implications of cryptography, we can foster a digital landscape that respects human dignity, mental well-being, and individual freedoms.

5.6 THE ETHICAL DILEMMA

Here are some actual events and cases that illustrate ethical dilemmas in information security and cryptography:

1. Apple vs. FBI (2016)

- **Event:** The FBI requested Apple's assistance in unlocking an iPhone used by one of the San Bernardino shooters. Apple resisted the request, stating that creating a back door to unlock the phone would compromise the security and privacy of all iPhone users.
- **Ethical Dilemma:** Balancing national security and law enforcement needs with user privacy and the potential precedent of creating back doors in encryption systems.

2. Heartbleed Vulnerability (2014)

- **Event:** The Heartbleed bug, a serious vulnerability in the OpenSSL cryptographic software library, was discovered. This bug exposed sensitive data, including usernames and passwords, on many websites.
- **Ethical Dilemma:** Coordinating the responsible disclosure of the vulnerability, as it required prompt patching by affected websites to protect users, but also posed a risk of exploitation if disclosed before fixes were widely implemented.

3. Stuxnet (2010)

- **Event:** Stuxnet was a sophisticated computer worm designed to target supervisory control and data acquisition (SCADA) systems. It is believed to have been developed by a nation–state to disrupt Iran's nuclear program.
- **Ethical Dilemma:** The use of advanced cyber weapons raises questions about the ethics of deploying malicious software for geopolitical purposes, as it can have unintended consequences and may set dangerous precedents.

4. NSA Surveillance Leaks by Edward Snowden (2013)

- **Event:** Edward Snowden, a former NSA contractor, leaked classified documents revealing the extensive surveillance programs conducted by the NSA, including the bulk collection of phone metadata.
- **Ethical Dilemma:** The disclosure raised ethical questions about the balance between national security interests and individual privacy, prompting a global debate on government surveillance practices.

5. Equifax Data Breach (2017)

- **Event:** Equifax, a major credit reporting agency, suffered a data breach that exposed the personal information of millions of individuals. The breach was due to a vulnerability that the company failed to patch promptly.
- **Ethical Dilemma:** The responsibility of organizations to promptly address known vulnerabilities to protect user data, and the ethical implications of failing to do so, leading to significant harm to individuals.

6. Hacking Team Breach (2015)

- **Event:** Hacking Team, an Italian cybersecurity firm, was hacked, and internal documents were leaked. These documents revealed the company's involvement in selling surveillance tools to governments with poor human rights records.
- **Ethical Dilemma:** The case highlighted the ethical concerns surrounding the sale of surveillance technology to repressive regimes and the responsibility of cybersecurity companies to consider the potential misuse of their products.

7. WannaCry Ransomware Attack (2017)

- **Event:** The WannaCry ransomware attack affected hundreds of thousands of computers worldwide, exploiting a vulnerability in Microsoft Windows. The vulnerability had been patched by Microsoft, but many systems remained unpatched.

- **Ethical Dilemma:** The incident underscored the ethical responsibility of organizations to promptly apply security patches to protect their systems and the potential consequences of failing to do so.

These real-world events illustrate the multifaceted ethical challenges in information security and cryptography, involving issues such as privacy, responsible disclosure, government surveillance, and the responsible development and use of cyber weapons.

5.6.1 The Ethical Tightrope: Balancing Security and Human Values

The widespread adoption of cryptographic technologies has brought forth a myriad of ethical considerations, challenging us to navigate the delicate balance between security imperatives and human values. As encryption becomes an integral part of our daily lives, we confront the ethical implications of its impact on privacy, free speech, and social justice.

The ethical implications of encryption are at the heart of a complex and contentious dilemma. The clash of perspectives revolves around the fundamental values of privacy, security, and individual rights, as well as the imperative to maintain public safety and protect society from potential harm.

From a privacy and civil liberties standpoint, encryption is viewed as an essential tool in upholding individual freedoms, enabling secure communication, and protecting sensitive data from unauthorized access. Advocates argue that strong encryption empowers individuals to exercise their rights to free speech, access information without fear of surveillance, and engage in secure online activities.

On the other side of the debate, security concerns drive the argument for exceptional access mechanisms that would allow authorized entities, such as law enforcement and intelligence agencies, to access encrypted data when necessary for legitimate purposes. The aim is to prevent criminal activities, safeguard public safety, and combat potential threats, even in the face of robust encryption.

The ethical dilemma lies in reconciling these contrasting perspectives and finding a path that respects both individual rights and public safety imperatives.

5.6.2 Privacy as a Fundamental Right

Privacy lies at the heart of the encryption debate, standing as a fundamental human right. The right to privacy fosters autonomy, self-determination, and the freedom to express oneself without fear of surveillance or intrusion.

Ethical cryptographic practices must prioritize privacy, resisting any attempts to weaken encryption for the sake of security. Striking a balance between safeguarding privacy and ensuring public safety is essential, upholding the principles of a democratic society that respects individual liberties.

5.6.3 Encryption and Social Justice

Encryption also plays a pivotal role in social justice efforts, empowering vulnerable populations to exercise their right to free speech and protect their identities from oppressive regimes or malicious actors.

In authoritarian regimes, secure communication channels enable dissidents, activists, and journalists to share critical information without fear of persecution. Ethical considerations dictate that we defend the right to encrypted communication, as it serves as a lifeline for those who seek to challenge injustices and advocate for positive societal change.

5.6.4 Digital Inclusion and Accessibility

Ensuring the ethical use of cryptographic technologies involves promoting digital inclusion and accessibility. As encryption becomes more integral to daily life, it is vital to bridge the digital divide, ensuring that marginalized communities have access to secure communication tools and education on responsible encryption practices.

Digital literacy and awareness campaigns can empower individuals to protect themselves from cyber threats while respecting their right to privacy. Ethical cryptographic policies must prioritize inclusivity, working towards a future where everyone can benefit from the protective powers of encryption.

5.6.5 Responsible Data Practices and Transparency

Ethical considerations extend beyond the development of cryptographic algorithms to encompass responsible data practices and transparency. Technology companies that offer encryption services must prioritize user privacy, ensuring that data is handled ethically and securely.

Transparent data practices build trust between users and service providers, fostering a relationship grounded in mutual respect and accountability. Ethical cryptographic technologies and policies should prioritize user agency, allowing individuals to have control over their data and make informed choices about their digital interactions.

5.6.6 Safeguarding Democracy and Digital Rights

In democratic societies, ethical cryptographic policies are essential to safeguarding democracy and upholding digital rights. By protecting the privacy of citizens, encryption ensures the free exchange of ideas, enabling robust public discourse and informed decision-making.

However, the ethical use of encryption should not obstruct legitimate law enforcement investigations or counterterrorism efforts. Striking a balance between these interests requires thoughtful and transparent policy-making that considers both security and human values.

5.6.7 Transparency, Accountability, and Responsible Encryption

To address the ethical dilemma of encryption, transparency and accountability are essential principles. Technology companies and encryption providers must be transparent about their data practices, encryption methodologies, and interactions with governments. This transparency builds trust among users and ensures that encryption systems are implemented responsibly.

Accountability extends to the responsible use of encryption by all stakeholders. Governments must be accountable for their surveillance activities and the scope of their requests for access to encrypted data. Technology companies must be accountable for protecting user data and resisting unwarranted or overly broad demands for access to encrypted communications.

Responsible encryption also involves a commitment to addressing vulnerabilities promptly and collaboratively. As encryption technologies evolve, stakeholders must work together to identify and mitigate potential risks to data security and privacy.

5.7 FINDING COMMON GROUND: ETHICAL CRYPTOGRAPHY PRINCIPLES

Finding common ground in the ethical dilemma of encryption requires the establishment of ethical cryptography principles that balance privacy, security, and individual rights.

These principles can serve as a foundation for responsible encryption practices that uphold both societal imperatives and democratic values.

Strong Encryption: Emphasize the importance of strong encryption to protect individual privacy and ensure data security against cyber threats.

Lawful Access: Advocate for responsible encryption practices that allow for lawful access to encrypted data in legitimate cases, subject to transparent and accountable processes.

User Consent: Respect user consent and privacy preferences, ensuring that individuals have the autonomy to make informed decisions about their data.

Transparency: Promote transparency in data practices, encryption methodologies, and interactions with governments to build trust among users.

Collaboration: Encourage collaboration among technology companies, governments, civil society, and academia to address encryption challenges and strike a balance between competing interests.

Human Rights: Uphold human rights principles, recognizing the importance of privacy, freedom of expression, and due process in the digital realm.

In this chapter, we have explored the ethical dimensions of cryptographic technologies and policies. Encryption stands at the intersection of security, privacy, and human values, necessitating careful consideration of its implications for society and democracy. Ethical cryptographic practices prioritize privacy, inclusivity, and transparency, striving to strike a harmonious balance between the protective powers of encryption and the preservation of individual rights and societal well-being. As we conclude our exploration, we reflect on the complex relationship between modern cryptography and humanity, seeking to shape a future where technology and human values coalesce in harmony.

The ethical dilemma of encryption is a complex issue that requires thoughtful consideration, collaboration, and a commitment to shared principles. As we navigate the evolving landscape of technology and privacy, responsible encryption practices grounded in transparency, accountability, and user empowerment can help reconcile competing perspectives.

By finding common ground and respecting the principles of privacy, security, and individual rights, we can shape a digital future that embraces the benefits of encryption while upholding the ethical values that define our democratic societies. Striking this balance will ensure that technology continues to serve humanity in ways that promote inclusivity, freedom, and the greater good for all.

Chapter 6

Anthropocentric Cryptography

6.1 FROM THE HEART

I feel like laughing when I hear phrases like "technological singularity" and upgrading human civilization over the Kardashev scale. Reason being, all such "scientific" jabberwocky is usually promoted by businesses. Business is about the real lives of real people. It is not a math problem to be solved nor is it about machines.

On a serious note, I believe that most of you would have heard of the "observer effect", wherein an electron can behave both like a particle or a wave depending upon whether it is being observed or not. What does this mean? Is it not indicative of some sort of "intelligence" embedded within the electron? i.e., it knows when it is being "observed" and accordingly

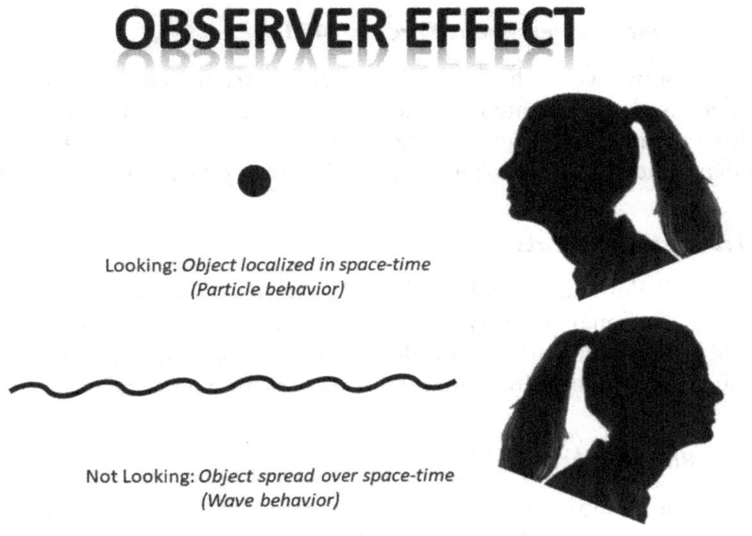

Looking: *Object localized in space-time*
(Particle behavior)

Not Looking: *Object spread over space-time*
(Wave behavior)

Figure 6.1 Observer Effect.

DOI: 10.1201/9781003527220-7

changes its behavior? So, where does this take us? *Doesn't it mean that the electron too is "observing" the "observer"?* That makes the "observer" the "observed". How can a fundamental tiny element turn the tables on us? It is this basic flaw of "modern science" that discounts the "observer", i.e., us humans in every experiment. The simplest example involves how we define our solar system—the heliocentric model. When you look at the heliocentric model—where are you looking at it from? Are you positioned millions of light years away from the solar system or are you part of it? In stark contrast, the geocentric model views the entire universe from locus standi, i.e., from our home planet Earth. Which model is more practical according to you?

Consider this—calculating the acceleration of a speeding car from the pit stop is not wrong but that doesn't help you any bit in the process of driving a car and for that you need to be in the driver's seat, i.e., inside the car! Doesn't that change your perspective? Likewise, designing complex machines and then making humans adapt to such machines is utterly foolish in every sense of the word. This is what is exactly meant when people discuss jargon like "singularity" and the Kardashev scale. There is a fundamental problem in this type of thought process.

6.1.1 Difficulty in Controlling Data Breaches

Data breaches are challenging to control due to various factors, including evolving technologies, human vulnerabilities, and the increasing sophistication of cybercriminals. Here are practical examples, use cases, and real-world events that illustrate the difficulties in controlling data breaches:

6.1.1.1 Advanced Persistent Threats (APTs)

The 2014 Sony Pictures hack involved an APT attributed to North Korea. The attackers used sophisticated techniques to infiltrate Sony's network, exfiltrate sensitive data, and disrupt operations. APTs often employ advanced tactics to remain undetected for extended periods, making them difficult to control.

6.1.1.2 Insider Threats

The case of Edward Snowden in 2013, who leaked classified information from the National Security Agency (NSA), highlights the challenges of dealing with insider threats. Insiders with legitimate access to systems can exploit their privileges, making it hard to prevent data breaches.

6.1.1.3 Phishing Attacks

In 2016, the Democratic National Committee (DNC) fell victim to a phishing attack, leading to the exposure of sensitive emails. Phishing remains a prevalent tactic where attackers use deceptive emails or messages to trick individuals into revealing confidential information.

6.1.1.4 Ransomware Attacks

The 2017 WannaCry ransomware attack affected organizations globally, exploiting vulnerabilities in outdated systems. Ransomware encrypts data and demands payment for decryption keys, making it challenging to recover data without cooperation from attackers.

6.1.1.5 Supply Chain Attacks

The SolarWinds cyberattack in 2020 involved compromising the software supply chain, leading to the infiltration of numerous government and private organizations. Attackers targeted a trusted vendor, making it difficult for organizations to detect malicious activities.

6.1.1.6 Cloud Security Challenges

Misconfigured cloud storage settings have led to several data breaches. In 2017, the personal data of millions of Verizon customers was exposed due to a misconfigured Amazon S3 bucket. The complexity of cloud environments increases the likelihood of misconfigurations.

6.1.1.7 Mobile Device Vulnerabilities

Mobile devices are often targeted due to their widespread use. In 2014, the Heartbleed vulnerability exposed sensitive information on Android devices. The diversity of mobile platforms and the large number of apps make it challenging to secure every endpoint effectively.

6.1.1.8 IoT (Internet of Things) Security Risks

In 2016, the Mirai botnet exploited insecure IoT devices to launch large-scale distributed denial-of-service (DDoS) attacks. The sheer number and diversity of IoT devices make it difficult to enforce security standards across the ecosystem.

6.1.1.9 Lack of Cybersecurity Awareness

Many data breaches result from human error, such as employees falling victim to social engineering attacks. Without proper cybersecurity awareness training, individuals may inadvertently compromise security, making it challenging to prevent breaches.

6.1.1.10 Regulatory Compliance Challenges

Organizations must comply with various data protection regulations. The complexity of staying compliant with different standards, such as GDPR or HIPAA, poses a challenge, and noncompliance can result in severe consequences.

These examples highlight the multifaceted nature of data breaches and underscore the importance of a holistic and proactive approach to cybersecurity. Controlling data breaches requires a combination of technological solutions, employee training, and a continuous effort to stay ahead of evolving threats.

6.1.2 Malicious / Bad Actors in Cryptography

Malicious actors, often referred to as "bad actors" or cybercriminals, play a central role in the challenges associated with data breaches. Their intent is to exploit vulnerabilities in systems, networks, and human behavior for various purposes, including unauthorized access, data theft, financial gain, and disruption of operations. Cryptography, while a crucial component of cybersecurity, has limitations in addressing certain aspects of the challenges posed by malicious actors:

6.1.2.1 Cryptography's Limitations against Human-Based Attacks

Cryptography is effective in securing data in transit and at rest. However, it cannot prevent all forms of social engineering and phishing attacks, where human manipulation is involved. Malicious actors often target individuals through deceptive tactics, tricking them into revealing sensitive information or credentials.

6.1.2.2 Key Management and Human Error

The effectiveness of many cryptographic systems relies on proper key management. Malicious actors often exploit human errors in key management, such as weak passwords, improper storage of keys, or accidental exposure. No matter how robust the cryptographic algorithms are, the human factor remains a vulnerability.

6.1.2.3 Zero-Day Exploits and Advanced Techniques

Cryptography can be rendered ineffective when attackers discover and exploit previously unknown vulnerabilities, known as zero-day exploits. Malicious actors, especially those involved in advanced persistent threats (APTs), continuously seek new ways to bypass cryptographic protections, such as leveraging undisclosed vulnerabilities or using sophisticated techniques like side-channel attacks.

6.1.2.4 Insider Threats and Authorized Access

Cryptography is less effective in situations where the threat comes from within an organization, as in the case of insider threats. If a malicious actor has legitimate access to cryptographic keys or sensitive data, encryption alone may not prevent unauthorized use or disclosure.

6.1.2.5 Ransomware and Encryption as a Double-Edged Sword

While encryption is a fundamental tool for protecting data, ransomware attacks leverage encryption as a weapon against organizations. Attackers use strong encryption to lock files, demanding payment for decryption keys. In this scenario, the cryptographic tools themselves become part of the threat landscape.

6.1.2.6 Quantum Computing Threats

The advent of quantum computing poses a potential threat to traditional cryptographic algorithms. Quantum computers, when sufficiently advanced, could break widely used encryption methods, leading to the need for quantum-resistant cryptographic solutions. The evolving landscape of quantum computing adds an additional layer of complexity to cryptographic defenses.

6.1.2.7 Supply Chain Attacks and Trusted Entities

Cryptography relies on the concept of trust in the entities providing cryptographic solutions. In supply chain attacks, malicious actors compromise trusted entities, introducing vulnerabilities into widely used cryptographic tools. This highlights the challenge of ensuring the integrity of the entire supply chain in the realm of cybersecurity.

In summary, while cryptography is a vital tool for securing information, it is not a panacea. It needs to be part of a broader cybersecurity strategy that includes measures to address human vulnerabilities, ongoing threat intelligence, and a comprehensive defense-in-depth approach. The role of malicious actors underscores the need for a dynamic and adaptive cybersecurity posture that goes beyond relying solely on cryptographic measures.

6.1.2.8 Modern Cryptography Is Not Human-Centric

User authentication is a critical aspect of cybersecurity, ensuring that individuals accessing systems, networks, or applications are who they claim to be. While modern cryptographic techniques play a significant role in securing authentication processes, they do have limitations when it comes to addressing human-centric issues. Here's how cryptographic techniques in user authentication can be less human-centric:

1. Password-Based Authentication

Challenge: Traditional password-based authentication relies on users creating and remembering strong passwords. However, human behavior often leads to the use of weak passwords, password reuse across multiple accounts, or the tendency to write down passwords, compromising the security of the authentication process.

Cryptographic Role: Cryptographic hash functions are used to securely store and verify passwords. However, if users choose weak passwords, the effectiveness of the cryptographic protection is compromised.

2. Multifactor Authentication (MFA)

Challenge: MFA adds an extra layer of security by combining something the user knows (password) with something the user has (e.g., a token or mobile device). However, the user experience can be affected, leading to potential resistance in adopting MFA.

Cryptographic Role: Cryptography is used to secure the transmission and verification of the additional authentication factors. However, the reliance on physical devices introduces a new set of challenges, such as the risk of device loss or malfunction.

3. Biometric Authentication

Challenge: Biometric authentication, such as fingerprint or facial recognition, is more user friendly, but it comes with privacy concerns. Biometric data, once compromised, cannot be easily replaced, and individuals may be hesitant to adopt these methods due to fears of unauthorized access or misuse.

Cryptographic Role: Cryptography is used to secure the storage and transmission of biometric data, but concerns regarding the centralized storage of sensitive biometric information persist.

4. Social Engineering Attacks

Challenge: Cryptographic methods alone cannot protect against social engineering attacks, where attackers manipulate individuals into revealing sensitive information or credentials. Human factors, such as trust and deception, play a significant role in the success of these attacks.

Cryptographic Role: While cryptography can secure the transmission and storage of authentication credentials, it cannot prevent users from being tricked into divulging this information through social engineering tactics.

5. Usability and User Experience

Challenge: Complex cryptographic methods can lead to poor usability and a negative user experience. Users may find it cumbersome to deal with frequent password changes, complex encryption processes, or the need for additional authentication factors.

Cryptographic Role: Cryptography aims to provide a secure framework, but if the user experience is overly complex, users may resort to insecure workarounds, defeating the purpose of robust cryptographic protocols.

6. Human Error in Key Management

Challenge: Cryptographic systems often require users to manage keys, and human error in key management can lead to vulnerabilities. Forgetting passwords, storing keys insecurely, or sharing credentials can compromise the security provided by cryptography.

Cryptographic Role: Cryptography relies on proper key management, and any failure in this regard can undermine the effectiveness of cryptographic techniques in user authentication.

6.1.3 Need for Change

To address these challenges, a holistic approach is necessary. Cryptographic techniques need to be complemented with user education, usability considerations, and continuous monitoring for anomalous behavior. Balancing security with user-friendly practices is crucial to developing authentication systems that are both effective and widely adopted.

To put it bluntly, the machines are made for us and not vice versa. For example, it's been over a century for mankind to be plying in vehicles. The most basic utility of a vehicle is its ability to transport us from one point to another at faster speeds. In general, we just want to drive it—there are specialists to repair it or maintain it. Fast forward to the 21st century, we are still struggling to develop an autonomous passenger vehicle both technologically and business-wise. Even if we succeed at it, we will still need humans to adapt to the requirements and in that process, we would lose our control of the very device that we consider a safe utility. What could we possibly do if it malfunctions? Even worse, what would be our predicament if it was to dictate our choices and define our eligibility to map our own journey?

Hence, without diverging further away, let me provide a glance into the gist of my postdoctoral thesis on information technology (IT) strategy viz. anthropocentric information security.

6.2 FROM THE HEAD

In the overall context of IT strategy, IT security holds an indispensable space that gets more and more complex as our technology, processes, and systems evolve. The different facets of IT security are shown here for a better understanding.

No matter what the function or the use case is, the entire gamut of IT security is based on cryptography. Cryptography is a subset of cryptology just like cryptanalysis is. In plain simple terms, the sole purpose of cryptography is to encrypt the data to prevent misuse across all stages like data generation, data acquisition, data transmission, data transformation, data analysis, data storage, and data destruction. Data retrieval is the antithesis and exception here.

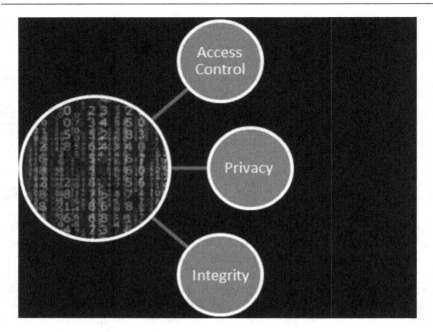

Figure 6.2 IT Strategy.

Without getting into the technical details of cryptography, most of us know that the process of encryption and decryption is performed automatically by machines (be it a microcontroller, a computer, or a supercomputer) with zero involvement from human beings in an ideal scenario (except while setting up policies or providing a key / pass phrase). Here, the original thought process is that since machines can perform complex calculations (e.g., processing of algorithms) faster than humans, it is appropriate to utilize them for encryption. As convenient as it may seem, humans will always have an upper hand as humans too can utilize machines to crack the encryption. Thus, no machine-encrypted data can be considered 100% safe and secure.

Now, if we look at the origins of cryptography without getting into the history of cryptology, we will realize that physical "ciphers" were used traditionally to safeguard any object / information. These ciphers usually had only one method of coding / decoding and were totally human centric, since there were no "intelligent machines" back then. It was almost impossible for a third person to decode the cipher without knowledge of the "secret key".

Figure 6.3 Ancient Cipher.

The basic difference between the origins of cryptography and modern algo-rithm-based cryptography is this:

1. *Machines can perform faster calculations than human beings, e.g., arithmetic operations*
2. *Humans surpass any known machine in cognitive intelligence, e.g., pattern recognition*

Modern cryptography is based on the first premise and totally ignores the second one. I intend to propose an anthropocentric cryptography based on the second premise. Such type of encryption / decryption would require humanlike cognitive intelligence and hence would be literally unbreakable by any machine. This is not an overstatement and can be demonstrated by the examples mentioned further in this book.

Chapter 7

ManusCrypt

7.1 HUMAN-CENTERED CRYPTOGRAPHY

"ManusCrypt" is a combination of "Manus" meaning human and "Crypt" meaning cipher; that denotes anthropocentric information security. It is my firm belief that any problem always has more than one solution. The solution proposed in this book is just one of the many. The focus is to find a solution that meets the human needs and not a mere solution for the sake of it.

So, before we venture into uncharted territories, let us understand the context behind the proposed solution.

7.1.1 Journey from Natural to Artificial

As can be seen from the previous figure, we can elucidate the effect of the transition:

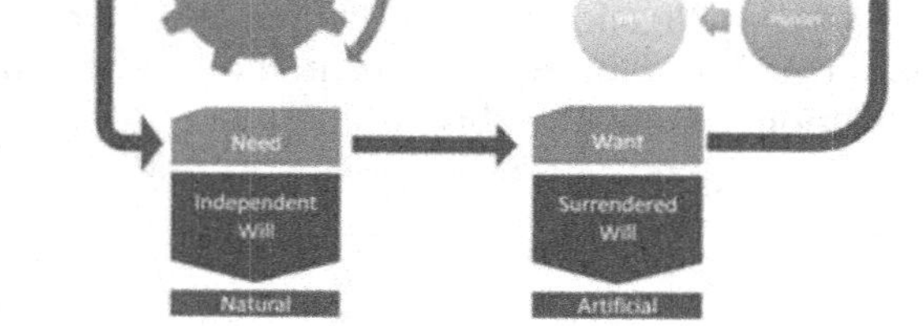

Figure 7.1 Journey from Natural to Artificial.

DOI: 10.1201/9781003527220-8

7.1.1.1 Natural Stage

Hunter felt hunger and went hunting. Will was negligible or driven by real need, i.e., hunger.

7.1.1.2 Intervention Stage

Gatherer sold a story and incentivized hunting. Gatherer captured the WILL of the hunter and the hunter is dependent on the incentives now.

7.1.1.3 Artificial Stage

Hunter is not willing to hunt until incentives are given and is ready to starve to death.

What was once a simplified process has now become a hijacked and complicated one, as the hunter is no longer willing to hunt without the promised incentives and is even willing to forego his own existence.

With this backdrop, one must think about the changing scenarios. We have indeed come a long way from the Caesar cipher to ECDSA, but at what price?

7.1.2 Natural Cryptography

Let us now try to understand what a human-centric cryptography would involve:

Table 7.1 Anthropocentric Information Security.

Sensory Faculty	Description	Ancient Examples	Modern Use Cases
Visual	Letters, numbers, symbols, shapes	Caesar cipher, Scytale cipher, etc.	iris-scan, passwords including steganography
Auditory	Speech or hearing based	Katapayadi Sutra	voice authentication, chatbots, AI assistants
Kinesthetic	Touch, task based	Tactile sensing in Abhinavgupta's Trankaloka	fingerprints, physical keys
Olfactory	Air, aroma based	Rasa Vayu Nidhi of Ayurveda	Glenlivet Cipher
Gustatory	Liquid, taste based	Rasa Jala Nidhi of Ayurveda	Glenlivet Cipher
Combinatorial	Combination of two or more of the aforementioned	Dhanurveda, Kautilya's Arthashastra	Nil

Modern cryptography is purely dependent on visual cues or abilities because everything gets interpreted by machines in the form of numbers alone, i.e., visual symbols. Why have the other four faculties been ignored?

While AR, VR, MR, haptics and similar technologies seem to address multiple sensory functions, they are still in their infancy and are not being intended to solve the problem of anthropocentric information security. Hence, a novel idea is being presented further to address the issue.

7.2 THE SOLUTION

In my proposal, I will be using a combination of the following for encrypting any given data via a user-generated "hash" function:

- "Steganography" (concealing the intended data within an image),
- "Sprouts game algorithm (SG)" $(3n - 1)$, and
- "Hasse Algorithm" / "Collatz conjecture (CC)" $(\{3n + 1\}/2)$

In simpler terms, I will be utilizing users' cognition to generate a unique hash function (viz. visual cue from an image), which will be then encrypted using two different algorithms.

Let me clarify that I'm not attempting to solve a mathematical problem or create a groundbreaking algorithm here. To put it simply, I'm attempting to shift the focus of cryptography from a machine-centered alphanumeric process to a human-centric process.

In this manner, the encryption and decryption process absolutely requires direct human involvement and cannot be breached by any machine at all.

The same can be explained using the game of chess:

Figure 7.2 Chessboard Gameplay.

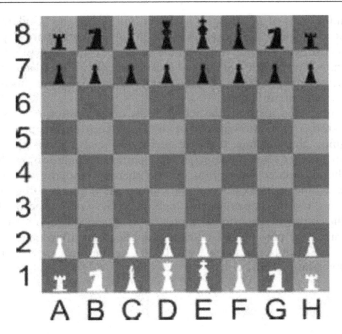

Figure 7.3 Chessboard Notation.

In Figures 7.2 and 7.3, we can see two images—the first one is the endgame with checkmate and the second one is the original chessboard configuration. Now, if one has to simulate the chess game in reverse one will have to visualize all the moves in a sequential order to reach the original chessboard configuration. For example, rook F7 to A1, queen A5 to D1, and so on. Now, a machine will have to calculate all the possible moves via an algorithm that will work out all the possible permutations and combinations for all 32 pieces across the 64 squares. In stark contrast, a human user just has to visually remember two squares—the original position and the final position for any random piece of his / her choice, in order to get authenticated. In this case, white bishop C1 to G4, only these two squares and the chosen piece needs to be remembered and selected by the user. The encryption / decryption that follows will be base64 in this case. If we consider the logarithmic base10, then we can have 1,764 routes to the original configuration, which are interspersed with several "infinite generation function" (IGF) elements. An intruder machine may compute the 1,764 routes at a great speed but will not be able to match the random IGF elements that are part of the user-generated hash function via CC. Thus, the code becomes unbreakable by any means. The only possible method is to replicate the user-generated hash by observing and copying the user actions on the same node—which will again be rejected due to duplication, as each attempt will be stored as a unique transaction over the network.

The uniqueness of my method is that it will utilize the "Collatz conjecture" (CC), which is a hundred-year-old unsolved mathematical problem, which in turn will provide unbreakable security to my encryption. Hence, even a brute-force attack will fail and unless someone can read a user's mind, the encryption cannot be breached. As long as the CC remains unsolved, my algorithm will remain intact.

In my proposed method, the whole basis of encryption / decryption is shifted to human cognition instead of any kind of arithmetic operation. This doesn't imply that machine-readable operations or algorithms are replaced. It only means that human cognition (e.g., pattern recognition) is placed on top of the automated encryption process thereby rendering it impossible for any machine to break the code in an automated manner. Regarding the implications and the impact of this method, if it is widely accepted, it will change the complete scenario of cryptography specifically and IT security in general, since the possible use-cases and applications are numerous. However, for ease of doing business I will be presenting a use case scenario for user authentication only.

## Chapter 8

Business Use Case Scenario

8.1 UTILITY

The application of "ManusCrypt" can be as varied as one's imagination. With certain modifications for proper implementation, it can cover everything from authentication to authorization and from data encryption to user access control. However, for ease of doing business we will cover only the following specific use-case scenario:

- User authentication for a web application
- Tool for client-side end-point security

Figure 8.1 User Authentication and End-Point Security.

8.2 USE CASE

As mentioned in the previous chapter, my method involves the use of these three concepts:

DOI: 10.1201/9781003527220-9

- Steganography
- Collatz conjecture
- Sprouts game algorithm

8.2.1 Collatz Conjecture or Hasse's Algorithm

The Collatz conjecture, also known as the $3n + 1$ conjecture, is an unsolved mathematical problem that is easy to understand but has baffled mathematicians for decades. It was introduced by the German mathematician Lothar Collatz in 1937.

The conjecture is defined as follows:
Start with any positive integer n.
If n is even, divide it by 2 to get $n/2$.
If n is odd, multiply it by 3 and add 1 to get $3n + 1$.

Repeat the process indefinitely with the newly obtained value, generating a sequence of numbers. The conjecture posits that, no matter what positive integer n you start with, the sequence will always reach the value 1 eventually.

Mathematically, the conjecture can be expressed using the following recurrence relation:

```
f(n) = {
n/2, if n is even,
3n + 1, if n is odd.
}
```

The Collatz conjecture has been verified for an incredibly large number of initial values, but no one has been able to prove that it holds true for all positive integers. In fact, the nature of the conjecture's behavior is not yet well understood, making it one of the most famous unsolved problems in mathematics.

Examples of the Collatz sequence:
Let's illustrate the Collatz sequence for a few initial values:

Starting with $n = 6$:
$6 \rightarrow 3 \rightarrow 10 \rightarrow 5 \rightarrow 16 \rightarrow 8 \rightarrow 4 \rightarrow 2 \rightarrow 1$
The sequence eventually reaches 1, which confirms the conjecture for $n = 6$.

Starting with $n = 19$:
$19 \rightarrow 58 \rightarrow 29 \rightarrow 88 \rightarrow 44 \rightarrow 22 \rightarrow 11 \rightarrow 34 \rightarrow 17 \rightarrow 52 \rightarrow 26 \rightarrow 13 \rightarrow 40 \rightarrow 20 \rightarrow 10 \rightarrow 5 \rightarrow 16 \rightarrow 8 \rightarrow 4 \rightarrow 2 \rightarrow 1$
The sequence also eventually reaches 1, which confirms the conjecture for $n = 19$.

Starting with $n = 27$:

$27 \rightarrow 82 \rightarrow 41 \rightarrow 124 \rightarrow 62 \rightarrow 31 \rightarrow 94 \rightarrow 47 \rightarrow 142 \rightarrow 71 \rightarrow 214 \rightarrow$
$107 \rightarrow 322 \rightarrow 161 \rightarrow 484 \rightarrow 242 \rightarrow 121 \rightarrow 364 \rightarrow 182 \rightarrow 91 \rightarrow 274 \rightarrow$
$137 \rightarrow 412 \rightarrow 206 \rightarrow 103 \rightarrow 310 \rightarrow 155 \rightarrow 466 \rightarrow 233 \rightarrow 700 \rightarrow 350 \rightarrow$
$175 \rightarrow 526 \rightarrow 263 \rightarrow 790 \rightarrow 395 \rightarrow 1{,}186 \rightarrow 593 \rightarrow 1{,}780 \rightarrow 890 \rightarrow 445$
$\rightarrow 1{,}336 \rightarrow 668 \rightarrow 334 \rightarrow 167 \rightarrow 502 \rightarrow 251 \rightarrow 754 \rightarrow 377 \rightarrow 1{,}132 \rightarrow$
$566 \rightarrow 283 \rightarrow 850 \rightarrow 425 \rightarrow 1{,}276 \rightarrow 638 \rightarrow 319 \rightarrow 958 \rightarrow 479 \rightarrow 1{,}438$
$\rightarrow 719 \rightarrow 2{,}158 \rightarrow 1{,}079 \rightarrow 3{,}238 \rightarrow 1{,}619 \rightarrow 4{,}858 \rightarrow 2{,}429 \rightarrow 7{,}288$
$\rightarrow 3{,}644 \rightarrow 1{,}822 \rightarrow 911 \rightarrow 2{,}734 \rightarrow 1{,}367 \rightarrow 4{,}102 \rightarrow 2{,}051 \rightarrow 6{,}154$
$\rightarrow 3{,}077 \rightarrow 9{,}232 \rightarrow 4{,}616 \rightarrow 2{,}308 \rightarrow 1{,}154 \rightarrow 577 \rightarrow 1{,}732 \rightarrow 866 \rightarrow$
$433 \rightarrow 1{,}300 \rightarrow 650 \rightarrow 325 \rightarrow 976 \rightarrow 488 \rightarrow 244 \rightarrow 122 \rightarrow 61 \rightarrow 184 \rightarrow$
$92 \rightarrow 46 \rightarrow 23 \rightarrow 70 \rightarrow 35 \rightarrow 106 \rightarrow 53 \rightarrow 160 \rightarrow 80 \rightarrow 40 \rightarrow 20 \rightarrow 10$
$\rightarrow 5 \rightarrow 16 \rightarrow 8 \rightarrow 4 \rightarrow 2 \rightarrow 1$

These examples demonstrate that for the given initial values, the sequences eventually reach the value 1. However, as of the end of 2023, the Collatz conjecture remains unproven for all positive integers, despite extensive computational evidence supporting it.

8.2.2 Python Code for Demonstration of Hasse's Algorithm

Hasse's algorithm, also known as the transitive reduction algorithm, is used to find the transitive reduction of a directed acyclic graph (DAG). The transitive reduction of a graph is a graph that contains the same reachability information as the original graph but has the fewest number of edges possible.

The algorithm works by iteratively removing edges that can be transitively reached from other edges without affecting reachability. The resulting graph is the transitive reduction.

Here's a Python implementation of Hasse's algorithm for a directed acyclic graph:

```python
def hasse_algorithm(graph):
    def dfs(node, visited):
        visited.add(node)
        for neighbor in graph.get(node, []):
            if neighbor not in visited:
                dfs(neighbor, visited)
```

```
    # Perform depth-first search from each node
    for node in list(graph.keys()):
      visited = set()
      dfs(node, visited)
      # Remove transitive edges
      for neighbor in list(graph.get(node, [])):
        if neighbor in visited:
          graph[node].remove(neighbor)

# Example DAG represented as an adjacency list
dag = {
  "A": ["B", "C"],
  "B": ["C", "D"],
  "C": ["D", "E"],
  "D": ["E"],
  "E": ["F", "G"],
  "F": ["G"],
  "G": [],
}

print("Original DAG:")
print(dag)
hasse_algorithm(dag)
print("\nTransitive Reduction:")
print(dag)
```

In this example, we use an adjacency list to represent the directed acyclic graph (DAG). The hasse_algorithm function performs a depth-first search (DFS) from each node in the graph, marking all reachable nodes. It then iterates through the neighbors of each node and removes the edge if the neighbor is reachable from the node. The resulting graph is the transitive reduction.

Output:

```
Original DAG:
{'A': ['B', 'C'], 'B': ['C', 'D'], 'C': ['D', 'E'], 'D':
['E'], 'E': ['F', 'G'], 'F': ['G'], 'G': []}

Transitive Reduction:
{'A': ['B'], 'B': ['C'], 'C': ['D'], 'D': ['E'], 'E':
['G'], 'F': ['G'], 'G': []}
```

As shown in the output, the transitive reduction of the original DAG is computed using Hasse's algorithm, resulting in the graph with the fewest number of edges while preserving reachability information.

8.2.2.1 Front-End Code for the Previous

Since Hasse's algorithm is a graph algorithm and doesn't involve user interactions, there is no direct front-end code for it. Front-end code is typically used for user interfaces and interaction with the user, while graph algorithms like Hasse's algorithm are more backend oriented and don't have a direct front-end representation.

However, if you want to visualize the graph and the transitive reduction generated by Hasse's algorithm, you can use a graph visualization library like NetworkX and Matplotlib. NetworkX is a Python library used for creating, analyzing, and visualizing complex networks, including directed acyclic graphs (DAGs).

Here's how you can visualize the graph and its transitive reduction using NetworkX and Matplotlib:

```python
import networkx as nx
import matplotlib.pyplot as plt
def hasse_algorithm(graph):
    #. . . Same hasse_algorithm function as before . . .

# Example DAG represented as an adjacency list
dag = {
    "A": ["B", "C"],
    "B": ["C", "D"],
    "C": ["D", "E"],
    "D": ["E"],
    "E": ["F", "G"],
    "F": ["G"],
    "G": [],
}

# Create a directed graph from the adjacency list
G = nx.DiGraph(dag)

# Draw the original graph
plt.figure(figsize=(8, 6))
pos = nx.spring_layout(G)
nx.draw(G, pos, with_labels=True, node_size=2000, node_
color="skyblue", font_size=12, font_weight="bold", edge_
color="gray", arrowsize=20)
```

```
plt.title("Original DAG")
plt.show()

# Apply Hasse's algorithm and draw the transitive reduc-
tion graph
hasse_algorithm(dag)
transitive_reduction_graph = nx.DiGraph(dag)

plt.figure(figsize=(8, 6))
pos = nx.spring_layout(transitive_reduction_graph)
nx.draw(transitive_reduction_graph,        pos,        with_
labels=True,   node_size=2000,   node_color="lightgreen",
font_size=12,   font_weight="bold",   edge_color="gray",
arrowsize=20)
plt.title("Transitive Reduction")
plt.show()
```

Before running the previous code, make sure you have installed Net-workX and Matplotlib using the following command:

```bash
bash

pip install networkx matplotlib
```

The code creates two visualizations: one for the original DAG and one for its transitive reduction. The nodes of the graph are displayed with labels, and the edges are shown as directed arrows. The original graph is displayed first, followed by the graph after applying Hasse's algorithm for transitive reduction.

Keep in mind that this visualization code is for demonstration purposes only and is not intended for large graphs. For larger and more complex graphs, you may need to explore specialized graph visualization tools or libraries.

8.2.2.2 API Code for Both Previous

Since Hasse's algorithm doesn't involve user interactions, the API code for it would be relatively simple. We'll create an API using Flask that exposes endpoints to receive a directed acyclic graph (DAG) as an adjacency list, apply Hasse's algorithm to find the transitive reduction, and return the result.

Create a Python file (e.g., api.py) and add the following code:

```
from flask import Flask, request, jsonify
import networkx as nx

app = Flask(__name__)

def hasse_algorithm(graph):
  G = nx.DiGraph(graph)
  transitive_reduction = nx.transitive_reduction(G)
  return transitive_reduction.adjacency()

@app.route("/transitive-reduction", methods=["POST"])
def transitive_reduction():
  data = request.json
  try:
     transitive_reduction_graph = hasse_algorithm(data)
     return jsonify(transitive_reduction_graph), 200
   except Exception as e:
     return jsonify({"error": str(e)}), 400

if __name__ == "__main__":
   app.run(debug=True)
```

In this API code, we define a single endpoint /transitive reduction that receives a directed acyclic graph (DAG) as an adjacency list in JSON format. The API applies Hasse's algorithm using NetworkX to find the transitive reduction and returns the resulting graph as an adjacency list in JSON format.

To test the API, you can use a tool like cURL, Postman, or any other REST API client. Alternatively, you can create a front end that sends a POST request to the transitive-reduction endpoint with the DAG data and receives the transitive reduction in response.

For testing purposes, you can use cURL from the command line:

```bash
curl -X POST -H "Content-Type: application/json" -d '{
  "A": ["B", "C"],
  "B": ["C", "D"],
  "C": ["D", "E"],
  "D": ["E"],
  "E": ["F", "G"],
  "F": ["G"],
  "G": []
  }' http://127.0.0.1:5000/transitive-reduction
```

The API should respond with the transitive reduction of the input DAG as an adjacency list in JSON format.

Please note that this example uses NetworkX to find the transitive reduction, which is a widely used library for graph-related operations in Python. If you are dealing with very large graphs, you may need to optimize the implementation or explore more specialized libraries. Additionally, the API code doesn't perform any input validation, error handling, or security measures, which should be added for a production-ready API.

8.2.3 "Sprouts Game Algorithm" with Worked-out Example

The Sprouts game is a two-player pen-and-paper game invented by John Horton Conway and Michael S. Paterson in 1967. The game is played on a sheet of paper using dots (called "spots") and lines (called "sprouts"). The objective of the game is to draw and extend lines (sprouts) between spots to create new spots while following specific rules. The game ends when no more sprouts can be drawn according to the rules. The player who draws the last sprout is declared the winner.

8.2.3.1 Rules of the Sprouts Game

The game starts with one or more spots (usually two or three).

On each turn, a player must draw a new sprout starting from an existing spot and ending at a new spot, following these rules:

 a. A new spot can be created at any position along the sprout, except at the starting or ending spot.
 b. Sprouts cannot intersect or overlap.
 c. A spot cannot have more than three sprouts extending from it.

The game ends when no more sprouts can be drawn according to the rules.
Let's go through a step-by-step example of playing the Sprouts game:

    Step 1: Start with two spots.
    . .
    Step 2: Player 1 draws the first sprout.
    . .
    \
    Step 3: Player 2 draws the second sprout.
    . .
    \ /
    Step 4: Player 1 extends the first sprout and creates a new spot.
    . .
    \ /.

Step 5: Player 2 extends the second sprout and creates a new spot.

```
. .
\ /.
\
```

Step 6: Player 1 extends the first sprout and creates a new spot.

```
. .
\ /.
. V
```

Step 7: Player 2 tries to extend the second sprout, but this violates the rule that a spot cannot have more than three sprouts. Since no more valid sprouts can be drawn, the game ends.

The final configuration of the game is:

```
. .
\ /.
. V.
\
```

Player 1 drew the last valid sprout and is declared the winner.

The Sprouts game is a challenging and interesting mathematical game with rich strategic possibilities. Since the game ends when no more valid sprouts can be drawn, players need to carefully plan their moves to block their opponent's potential sprouts and create opportunities to extend their own sprouts.

8.2.4 Sprouts Game in Python

8.2.4.1 Backend Code in Python

Implementing the Sprouts game in Python requires creating a graphical interface to draw and extend the sprouts. For this example, we'll use the pygame library, which provides tools for creating simple 2D games and graphical applications.

First, make sure you have installed pygame:

```
pip install pygame
Next, create a Python file (e.g., sprouts_game.py) and add
the following code:


python


import pygame
import sys
```

```python
# Initialize pygame
pygame.init()

# Constants
SCREEN_WIDTH, SCREEN_HEIGHT = 800, 600
BACKGROUND_COLOR = (255, 255, 255) # White
DOT_COLOR = (0, 0, 0) # Black
SPROUT_COLOR = (0, 0, 255) # Blue
DOT_RADIUS = 5

# Store spots and sprouts
spots = [(100, 100), (600, 100)] # Start with two spots
sprouts = []

# Create the game window
screen    =    pygame.display.set_mode((SCREEN_WIDTH,
SCREEN_HEIGHT))
pygame.display.set_caption("Sprouts Game")

def draw_game():
  # Draw the background
  screen.fill(BACKGROUND_COLOR)

  # Draw the spots
  for spot in spots:
    pygame.draw.circle(screen, DOT_COLOR, spot, DOT_RADIUS)

  # Draw the sprouts
  for sprout in sprouts:
    pygame.draw.line(screen, SPROUT_COLOR, sprout[0],
sprout[1], 2)

  # Update the display
  pygame.display.flip()

def add_sprout(start_spot, end_spot):
  # Check if the sprout is valid
  if (end_spot not in spots and len(get_connected_
sprouts(end_spot)) < 3):
      sprouts.append((start_spot, end_spot))
      spots.append(end_spot)

def get_connected_sprouts(spot):
  connected_sprouts = []
```

```
  for sprout in sprouts:
    if sprout[0] == spot:
      connected_sprouts.append(sprout)
    elif sprout[1] == spot:
        connected_sprouts.append((sprout[1], sprout[0]))
# Reverse the sprout direction
  return connected_sprouts

def main():
  running = True
  while running:
    for event in pygame.event.get():
      if event.type == pygame.QUIT:
        running = False
      elif event.type == pygame.MOUSEBUTTONDOWN:
        if event.button == 1: # Left mouse button click
          mouse_pos = pygame.mouse.get_pos()
          for spot in spots:
            dist = ((spot[0]-mouse_pos[0]) ** 2 +
(spot[1]-mouse_pos[1]) ** 2) ** 0.5
            if dist < DOT_RADIUS:
              connected = get_connected_sprouts(spot)
              if len(connected) < 3:
                add_sprout(spot, mouse_pos)
                draw_game()

  pygame.quit()
  sys.exit()

if __name__ == "__main__":
  main()
```

This code sets up a basic graphical interface using pygame to draw the spots and sprouts. You can interact with the game by clicking the left mouse button on a spot, and it will extend a sprout to a new spot.

Please note that this implementation is for educational purposes and provides only a basic graphical interface. For a more polished and interactive game, you may want to implement additional features, such as player turns, victory conditions, and more sophisticated user interactions. Additionally, this example does not include any validation for user input, so you should be cautious not to break the game's rules (e.g., exceeding the maximum number of sprouts per spot).

8.2.4.2 Front-End Code for the Previous

To create the front-end code for the Sprouts Game, we'll use HTML, CSS, and JavaScript. We'll create an HTML canvas where the game will be displayed and use JavaScript to handle user interactions and communicate with the backend (server) code that we previously implemented in Python.

Here's the front-end code for the Sprouts Game:

Create an HTML file (e.g., index.html) and add the following code:

```
<!DOCTYPE html>
<html lang="en">
<head>
 <meta charset="UTF-8">
 <meta name="viewport" content="width=device-width,
initial-scale=1.0">
 <title>Sprouts Game</title>
 <style>
  canvas {
  border: 1px solid black;
  }
 </style>
</head>
<body>
 <canvas id="gameCanvas" width="800" height="600"></canvas>
 <script src="frontend.js"></script>
</body>
</html>
Create a JavaScript file (e.g., frontend.js) and add the
following code:
javascript

const canvas = document.getElementById("gameCanvas");
const ctx = canvas.getContext("2d");

const SPRITE_RADIUS = 5;
const SPROUT_COLOR = "blue";

let spots = [];
let sprouts = [];

// Function to draw spots and sprouts on the canvas
function drawGame() {
ctx.clearRect(0, 0, canvas.width, canvas.height);

// Draw the spots
 for (let spot of spots) {
```

```
  ctx.beginPath();
  ctx.arc(spot[0], spot[1], SPRITE_RADIUS, 0, Math.PI * 2);
  ctx.fillStyle = "black";
  ctx.fill();
  ctx.closePath();
 }

 // Draw the sprouts
 for (let sprout of sprouts) {
  ctx.beginPath();
  ctx.moveTo(sprout[0][0], sprout[0][1]);
  ctx.lineTo(sprout[1][0], sprout[1][1]);
  ctx.strokeStyle = SPROUT_COLOR;
  ctx.lineWidth = 2;
  ctx.stroke();
  ctx.closePath();
 }
}

// Function to handle user clicks on the canvas
function handleCanvasClick(event) {
 const rect = canvas.getBoundingClientRect();
 const mouseX = event.clientX-rect.left;
 const mouseY = event.clientY-rect.top;

 // Check if the click is within a spot
  for (let spot of spots) {
    const dist = Math.sqrt((spot[0]-mouseX) ** 2 + (spot[1]-
mouseY) ** 2);
    if (dist < SPRITE_RADIUS) {
    // Prompt the user to draw a new sprout
    const newSpotX = prompt("Enter X coordinate of the
new spot:");
    const newSpotY = prompt("Enter Y coordinate of the new
spot:");
    if (newSpotX && newSpotY) {
     const newSpot = [parseInt(newSpotX), parseInt
(newSpotY)];
     if (!spots.find((spot) => spot[0] === newSpot[0] &&
spot[1] === newSpot[1])) {
       // Add the new spot and sprout
       sprouts.push([spot, newSpot]);
       spots.push(newSpot);
       drawGame();
     } else {
       alert("Spot already exists!");
     }
```

```
        }
      break;
      }
    }
  }
}

// Attach the event listener for canvas clicks
canvas.addEventListener("click", handleCanvasClick);

// Initial configuration for testing
spots = [[100, 100], [600, 100]];
sprouts = [[[100, 100], [200, 100]], [[600, 100], [700,
100]]];

// Draw the initial game state
drawGame();
```

In this front-end code, we create an HTML canvas with a correspond-ing JavaScript file to handle user interactions. The drawGame function is responsible for drawing the spots and sprouts on the canvas. The handle-CanvasClick function listens for user clicks and prompts the user to enter the coordinates of the new spot when clicking on an existing spot.

You can use this front-end code by saving the HTML and JavaScript code into separate files (index.html and frontend.js, respectively) and opening the index.html file in a web browser. The initial configuration of spots and sprouts can be modified or replaced with the actual game state from the server.

Remember that this front-end code only handles user interactions and displays the game's state on the canvas. It does not include any communica-tion with the server, which would be required for a complete multiplayer implementation. Additionally, there is no validation or error handling for user input in this example, so you should add proper validation and error handling for a more robust application.

8.2.4.3 API Code in Python

We'll use the Flask web framework again to create the API for the Sprouts game. The API will handle user interactions, maintain the game state, and communicate with the front end using JSON data.

Create a Python file (e.g., api.py) and add the following code:

```python
from flask import Flask, request, jsonify

app = Flask(__name__)

# Store spots and sprouts
spots = [(100, 100), (600, 100)] # Start with two spots
sprouts = [[[100, 100], [200, 100]], [[600, 100], [700,
100]]]

def add_sprout(start_spot, end_spot):
  # Check if the sprout is valid
  if (end_spot not in spots and len(get_connected_
sprouts(end_spot)) < 3):
   sprouts.append([start_spot, end_spot])
   spots.append(end_spot)

def get_connected_sprouts(spot):
  connected_sprouts = []
  for sprout in sprouts:
    if sprout[0] == spot:
      connected_sprouts.append(sprout)
    elif sprout[1] == spot:
       connected_sprouts.append([sprout[1], sprout[0]])
# Reverse the sprout direction
   return connected_sprouts

@app.route("/game", methods=["GET"])
def get_game_state():
  return jsonify({"spots": spots, "sprouts": sprouts})

@app.route("/game/sprout", methods=["POST"])
def add_sprout_endpoint():
  data = request.json
  start_spot = tuple(data.get("start_spot"))
  end_spot = tuple(data.get("end_spot"))

  if not start_spot or not end_spot:
     return jsonify({"message": "Invalid data."}), 400

  add_sprout(start_spot, end_spot)
  return jsonify({"message": "Sprout added success-
fully."}), 201

if __name__ == "__main__":
   app.run(debug=True)
```

In this API code, we use Flask to define two endpoints:

/game: This endpoint returns the current game state, including the spots and sprouts. It is used to initialize the front end and synchronize the game state between the front end and backend.

/game/sprout: This endpoint receives data from the front end with the coordinates of the new sprout and adds it to the game state. It returns a response indicating whether the sprout was added successfully.

To communicate with the front end, you need to modify the JavaScript code from the front-end example. Update the handleCanvasClick function to send the new sprout data to the server and fetch the updated game state. Replace the front-end JavaScript code with the following:

```javascript
const canvas = document.getElementById("gameCanvas");
const ctx = canvas.getContext("2d");

const SPRITE_RADIUS = 5;
const SPROUT_COLOR = "blue";

let spots = [];
let sprouts = [];

// Function to draw spots and sprouts on the canvas
function drawGame() {
 ctx.clearRect(0, 0, canvas.width, canvas.height);

// Draw the spots
 for (let spot of spots) {
  ctx.beginPath();
  ctx.arc(spot[0], spot[1], SPRITE_RADIUS, 0, Math.PI * 2);
  ctx.fillStyle = "black";
  ctx.fill();
  ctx.closePath();
 }

// Draw the sprouts
 for (let sprout of sprouts) {
  ctx.beginPath();
  ctx.moveTo(sprout[0][0], sprout[0][1]);
  ctx.lineTo(sprout[1][0], sprout[1][1]);
  ctx.strokeStyle = SPROUT_COLOR;
  ctx.lineWidth = 2;
  ctx.stroke();
  ctx.closePath();
```

```
    }
}

// Function to handle user clicks on the canvas
function handleCanvasClick(event) {
  const rect = canvas.getBoundingClientRect();
  const mouseX = event.clientX—rect.left;
  const mouseY = event.clientY—rect.top;

  // Check if the click is within a spot
  for (let spot of spots) {
    const dist = Math.sqrt((spot[0]—mouseX) ** 2 + (spot[1]—
mouseY) ** 2);
    if (dist < SPRITE_RADIUS) {
      // Prompt the user to draw a new sprout
      const newSpotX = prompt("Enter X coordinate of the
new spot:");
      const newSpotY = prompt("Enter Y coordinate of the
new spot:");
      if (newSpotX && newSpotY) {
        const newSpot = [parseInt(newSpotX), parseInt
(newSpotY)];
        if (!spots.find((spot) => spot[0] === newSpot[0]
&& spot[1] === newSpot[1])) {
        // Send the new sprout data to the server
        fetch("/game/sprout", {
         method: "POST",
         headers: {
          "Content-Type": "application/json",
         },
         body: JSON.stringify({
          start_spot: spot,
          end_spot: newSpot,
         }),
        })
          .then((response) => response.json())
          .then((data) => {
           if (data.message === "Sprout added successfully.") {
            // Fetch the updated game state from the server
             fetch("/game")
               .then((response) => response.json())
               .then((data) => {
                spots = data.spots;
                sprouts = data.sprouts;
                drawGame();
               });
```

```
      } else {
        alert(data.message);
      }
    });
  } else {
    alert("Spot already exists!");
  }
 }
}
  break;
 }
 }
}


// Attach the event listener for canvas clicks
canvas.addEventListener("click", handleCanvasClick);

// Fetch the initial game state from the server
fetch("/game")
  .then((response) => response.json())
  .then((data) => {
    spots = data.spots;
    sprouts = data.sprouts;
    drawGame();
  });
```

This front-end JavaScript code sends the new sprout data to the server using the /game/sprout endpoint and fetches the updated game state from the server using the /game endpoint after a new sprout is added.

With the front-end and backend (API) code in place, you should be able to play the Sprouts game by opening the index.html file in your web browser. The front end will display the game's state, and you can interact with the game by clicking on existing spots and adding new sprouts according to the game's rules. The game state will be synchronized between the front end and backend through the API endpoints.

8.2.5 Python Code for Cryptographic Function Based on Steganography

Steganography is the practice of concealing secret information within a carrier medium, such as an image, audio file, or video, without changing the apparent properties of the carrier medium. In this example, I'll show you a simple implementation of a cryptographic function based on steganography using Python to hide and retrieve a secret message within an image. We'll use the Python Imaging Library (PIL) to work with images.

Before running the code, make sure to install the Pillow library, which is an actively maintained fork of PIL:

```
pip install Pillow
Here's the Python code for the cryptographic function:

python

from PIL import Image

def encode_message(image_path, message):
  image = Image.open(image_path)

  # Convert the message to binary
  binary_message = ".join(format(ord(char), '08b') for
char in message)

  if len(binary_message) > image.width * image.height:
      raise ValueError("Message is too long to encode in
the image.")

  encoded_pixels = []
  binary_index = 0

  for pixel in image.getdata():
    r, g, b = pixel
    # Encode the message into the least significant bit
of each color channel
    encoded_pixel = (r & ~1, g & ~1, b & ~1)

    if binary_index < len(binary_message):
        # Replace the least significant bit with the binary
message
        encoded_pixel = (
        r | int(binary_message[binary_index]),
        g | int(binary_message[binary_index + 1]),
        b | int(binary_message[binary_index + 2]),
        )
        binary_index += 3

    encoded_pixels.append(encoded_pixel)

  # Create a new image with the encoded pixels
  encoded_image = Image.new("RGB", image.size)
  encoded_image.putdata(encoded_pixels)
```

```
        encoded_image.save("encoded_image.png")
        print("Message encoded and saved in 'encoded_image.
png'.")

def decode_message(encoded_image_path):
    encoded_image = Image.open(encoded_image_path)
    binary_message = "

    for pixel in encoded_image.getdata():
        # Extract the least significant bit from each color channel
        r, g, b = pixel
        binary_message += str(r & 1)
        binary_message += str(g & 1)
        binary_message += str(b & 1)

    message = "
    for i in range(0, len(binary_message), 8):
        # Convert binary to ASCII characters
        byte = binary_message[i:i + 8]
        message += chr(int(byte, 2))

    return message

# Example usage
image_path = "sample_image.png"
message_to_hide = "Hello, this is a secret message!"

# Encode the message in the image
encode_message(image_path, message_to_hide)

# Decode the message from the encoded image
decoded_message = decode_message("encoded_image.png")
print("Decoded Message:", decoded_message)
```

In this implementation, the encode_message function takes an image path and a secret message as input. The function converts the message to binary and encodes it into the least significant bit of each color channel (RGB) of the image. The decode_message function takes the path of the encoded image and retrieves the hidden message by extracting the least significant bit of each color channel.

Please note that this example provides a simple demonstration of steganography. In real-world applications, more advanced techniques and precautions are needed to ensure the security and robustness of the hidden message.

8.2.6 Infinite Generation Function

An "infinite generation function" refers to a function or algorithm that can produce an infinite sequence of elements or values continuously without reaching an end. These functions are often used in various computational scenarios where an unbounded or potentially limitless sequence of data is required or useful. Infinite generation functions are particularly common in the context of mathematics, computer science, and data processing.

Here are some key characteristics and properties of an infinite generation function:

Continuous Output: An infinite generation function continuously generates output without stopping or reaching a limit. The function may be designed to generate values one by one or produce an unending stream of data.

Lazy Evaluation: In some cases, an infinite generation function may employ "lazy evaluation", meaning that it only generates elements of the sequence as they are needed or requested. This approach allows for more efficient memory utilization and avoids generating unnecessary data up front.

Infinite Domain: Infinite generation functions often operate over an infinite domain, meaning that the set of possible inputs or values is infinite or unbounded. For example, the sequence of natural numbers $(1, 2, 3, \ldots)$ is an infinite domain.

Iterative or Recursive Algorithms: Infinite generation functions are typically implemented using iterative or recursive algorithms that allow them to generate elements indefinitely. These algorithms may be based on mathematical formulas, recursive rules, or dynamic programming techniques.

Examples: Infinite generation functions can be found in various mathematical sequences, such as the Fibonacci sequence, prime numbers, and geometric progressions. In computer science, they are used in generating random numbers, processing infinite data streams, and solving certain computational problems.

Termination Condition (Optional): In some cases, an infinite generation function may have an optional termination condition. This allows the function to stop generating elements when a certain criterion is met or when the user decides to terminate the process.

8.2.7 IGF in Python

Here's a simple example of an infinite generation function in Python using a generator function to generate an infinite sequence of natural numbers:

```
def natural_numbers():
  num = 1
  while True:
   yield num
   num += 1

# Create an instance of the generator function
generator = natural_numbers()

# Generate and print the first 10 natural numbers
for _ in range(10):
  print(next(generator))
```

In this example, the natural_numbers generator function generates an infinite sequence of natural numbers (1, 2, 3, . . .). The yield statement allows the function to produce the next number in the sequence when requested using the next() function.

It's essential to use infinite generation functions with caution, as they can consume significant computational resources and memory if not managed appropriately. In some cases, it may be necessary to apply termination conditions or use lazy evaluation to control the generation process effectively.

8.2.7.1 Popular Infinite Generation Functions

An infinite generation function (IGF) generates an infinite sequence of values. Since we cannot list an infinite sequence explicitly, I can provide you with a few examples of IGFs and their behavior for values from 1 to 10.

8.2.7.1.1 Fibonacci Sequence

The Fibonacci sequence is a well-known infinite generation function defined by the recurrence relation: $F(n) = F(n-1) + F(n-2)$ with initial values $F(0) = 0$ and $F(1) = 1$. The sequence goes on indefinitely, generating values by adding the two previous terms.

> **Example:** The first ten values of the Fibonacci sequence are [0, 1, 1, 2, 3, 5, 8, 13, 21, 34].

8.2.7.1.2 Prime Numbers

The set of prime numbers is another example of an infinite generation function. Prime numbers are natural numbers greater than 1 that have no divisors other than 1 and themselves.

Example: The first ten prime numbers are [2, 3, 5, 7, 11, 13, 17, 19, 23, 29].

8.2.7.1.3 Natural Numbers

The simplest infinite generation function is the set of natural numbers, which includes all positive integers starting from 1.

Example: The first ten natural numbers are [1, 2, 3, 4, 5, 6, 7, 8, 9, 10].

8.2.7.1.4 Powers of 2

The sequence of powers of 2 is an infinite generation function that grows exponentially.

Example: The first ten powers of 2 are [2, 4, 8, 16, 32, 64, 128, 256, 512, 1,024].

8.2.7.1.5 Factorial Numbers

The factorial function generates an infinite sequence of values by multiplying natural numbers from 1 to n.

Example: The first ten factorial numbers are [1, 2, 6, 24, 120, 720, 5,040, 40,320, 362,880, 3,628,800].

8.2.7.1.6 Natural Logarithm (ln(x))

The natural logarithm is the inverse function of the exponential function. It generates an infinite sequence of real numbers for positive input values.

Example: The values of $\ln(x)$ for x from 1 to 10 (rounded to four decimal places) are [0.0000, 0.6931, 1.0986, 1.3863, 1.6094, 1.7918, 1.9459, 2.0794, 2.1972, 2.3026].

8.2.7.1.7 Exponential Function (e^x)

The exponential function generates an infinite sequence of real numbers for any real input x.

Example: The values of e^x for x from 1 to 10 (rounded to four decimal places) are [2.7183, 7.3891, 20.0855, 54.5982, 148.4132, 403.4288, 1096.6332, 2980.9580, 8103.0839, 22026.4658].

8.2.7.1.8 Sine Function (sin(x))

The sine function generates an infinite sequence of values between –1 and 1 for any real input x.

> **Example:** The values of sin(x) for x from 1 to 10 (rounded to four decimal places) are [0.8415, 0.1411, –0.9589, –0.5440, 0.6561, 0.4121, –0.9894, –0.5440, 0.8930, –0.8391].

8.2.7.1.9 Cosine Function (cos(x))

The cosine function generates an infinite sequence of values between –1 and 1 for any real input x.

> **Example:** The values of cos(x) for x from 1 to 10 (rounded to four decimal places) are [0.5403, –0.9899, –0.2837, 0.8391, 0.7539, –0.9111, –0.1455, 0.9998, 0.5291, –0.8391].

8.2.7.1.10 Square Root (sqrt(x))

The square root function generates an infinite sequence of real numbers for positive input values.

> **Example:** The values of sqrt(x) for x from 1 to 10 (rounded to four decimal places) are [1.0000, 1.4142, 1.7321, 2.0000, 2.2361, 2.4495, 2.6458, 2.8284, 3.0000, 3.1623].

Please note that these examples provide sequences of values for the specified functions from 1 to 10. However, these sequences continue indefinitely, generating an infinite number of values beyond the range mentioned here.

8.3 PROOF OF CONCEPT

When we combine the previously stated three methods into one single executable code, what we get is a tool that renders an "unbreakable" password. Let me explain it further here:

- **Steganographic Function:** This facilitates the user to perform an image-based task without having to physically key in the password. The user input is stored as a hash function for further processing.
- **Infinite Generation Function (IGF):** This generates infinite generation function based on custom tables and provides a set of values to match with the user generated hash function thus generating infinite computing options.

- **Sprouts Game Function (SGF):** This interacts with the user input to provide an element of randomness and conveys the validity to the next function.
- **Collatz Conjecture Function (CCF):** This translates the validation from the previous function to the core algorithm and locks in to the value generated from the earlier functions thus providing uniqueness of operation.

In this manner, even if brute-force attack is employed, the attacker machine will be directed into an infinite loop of IGFs, technically leading it into the classical halting problem.

8.4 USER EXPERIENCE

It is imperative to describe the user experience, in order to provide a complete view of the solution.

As shown shortly, after the initial one-time registration the user log-in prompt will be replaced by an image (more on the image in the next chapter), where the user only has to perform a simple task in a random manner:

Figure 8.2 RAM User Interface.

The technology you use impresses no one, the experience you create with it is everything.
- Sean Gerety

Figure 8.3 Sean Gerety Quote.

For example, let the user select arrow #3 to hit head #7. Note that the user has to just perform two clicks to select the variables in the image. The password need not be keyed in and the image-based task will get encoded into a hash function. The user generated hash value and the corresponding value from the custom IGF table will form a pair and be logged as a unique transaction.

That's it! The user need not key in or even remember the password for *n* number of attempts as decided during the initial one-time registration. All that the user needs to do is perform an image-based task and remember that particular task (two clicks on the image) only for that session.

Sean Gerety's quote succinctly captures the essence of the relationship between technology and human experience. In a world inundated with technological advancements, it's easy to become fixated on the capabilities and specifications of the tools we use. However, Gerety reminds us that the true value lies not in the technology itself, but rather in the experiences it facilitates. In essence, the quote underscores the importance of how technology is utilized to enhance human interactions, solve problems, and create meaningful experiences. No matter how cutting edge or impressive a piece of technology may be, its impact ultimately hinges on the experiences it enables or enhances for individuals or communities.

This perspective is particularly relevant in fields like design, marketing, and customer service, where the focus should be on crafting experiences that resonate with people on an emotional level. It also emphasizes the need for empathy and understanding of human needs and desires in the development and implementation of technology. In the current context, this quote highlights the need to redesign the gamut of information security vis-à-vis humanistic design. Stuff like FHE and quantum computing might sound superior in terms of advancement of technology but do they cater to the innate needs of the average user?

(Source of quote: https://blog.mastek.com/experience-is-everything-wealth-management)

Chapter 9

RAM for ManusCrypt

9.1 CUSTOM SOURCE

Based on the outlines presented in the previous chapter, a table of infinite generation function can be prepared. There can be several IGF tables and one such IGF table has been presented here derived from "Ravana's algorithmic matrix" (RAM). Unlike the IGFs as per traditional mathematics (prime numbers, Fibonacci sequence, etc.), this table has its roots in the great Indian epic of Ramayana.

Ravana, the demon king, had acquired a boon that he would get ten heads for each severed head, since he had offered his head ten times to Lord Brahma during penance. Fast forward to the final battle between Lord Rama and Ravana. Lord Rama was unable to defeat Ravana, as with each severed head, ten heads would appear again. Now, this is just a passing reference in the great epic, which eventually has a happy ending where good wins over evil, as Lord Rama slays Ravana through breaking his secret. The real secret for us lies in Ravana's boon—for every severed head, ten heads would appear. I would not shy away from saying that, it is Lord Rama who actually generated the RAM in the process of trying in every possible way to behead Ravana.

Denoting it mathematically, we have:

$X = 1 \rightarrow \infty$ "X" representing Ravana's head
$Y = 1 \rightarrow 10$ severing of Ravana's head in one attempt
$Z = 10$ ten heads replacing one severed head each time
$n = 1 \rightarrow \infty$ number of attempts

Now we have,

$X_1 = (X_0 - Y_0) + (Z * X_0)$ where,
$X_0 = 1, Y_0 = 1$

DOI: 10.1201/9781003527220-10

To get the total count of heads after each attempt we have,

$$X_2 = (X_1 - Y_1) + (10 * X_1)$$
$$X_3 = (X_2 - Y_2) + (10 * X_2)$$
$$X_{n+1} = (X_n - Y_n) + (10 * X_n)$$
$$X_{\infty+1} = (X_\infty - Y_\infty) + (10 * X_\infty)$$

For example, when only one head is severed in the first attempt,

$$X_1 = (1 - 1) + (10 * 1) = 10$$

So, for ten heads in the second attempt, we have

$$X_2 = (10 - 10) + (10 * 10) = 100$$

Likewise, for the tenth attempt we can have

$$X_{10} = (397 - 3) + (10 * 3) = 424$$

where the value of "X_{n+1}" can differ based on the value X_n from previous attempts. So, for the given example we can have the following table:

Table 9.1 IGF Table 1.

n	Y_n	X_n
1	1	10
2	10	100
3	7	163
4	1	172
5	4	208
6	6	262
7	2	280
8	5	325
9	8	397
10	3	424

Now, going back to the chosen user input as mentioned in the previous chapter, we can also have the following table that meets our needs:

Table 9.2 IGF Table 2.

n	Y_n	X_n
1	1	10
2	5	55
3	7	118
4	1	127
5	4	163
6	6	217
7	2	235
8	5	280
9	8	352
10	3	379

Likewise, for the chosen user input we can have,

Xn = 82, 91, 100, 109, 118, 127, 136, 145, 154, 163 for n = 10
(termination condition).

So, in an ideal condition where $n = \infty$, we have an IGF as a result of the simple input of the user.

The sequence of severing the heads may vary from one head at a time to all ten heads simultaneously. So, we have the following table for reference:

Now, Xn = 82 → 973 for n = 100

This way for the chosen user input, the IGF table value can assume any of the 100 different values.

9.2 CRYPTOGRAPHIC FUNCTION

Now that RAM for ManusCrypt has been understood, let us try to gain an insight into the cryptographic function of the same.

As mentioned in the PoC in the previous chapter, out of the IGF table values arrived at from the user input (as shown in Figure 8.2) a random value from the IGF (refer Tables 9.1, 9.2, and Figure 9.1) is selected via the SGF, and then converted into a hash.

For example, for Xn = 82 → 973, we have
Xn = X_{66} = 667 so,

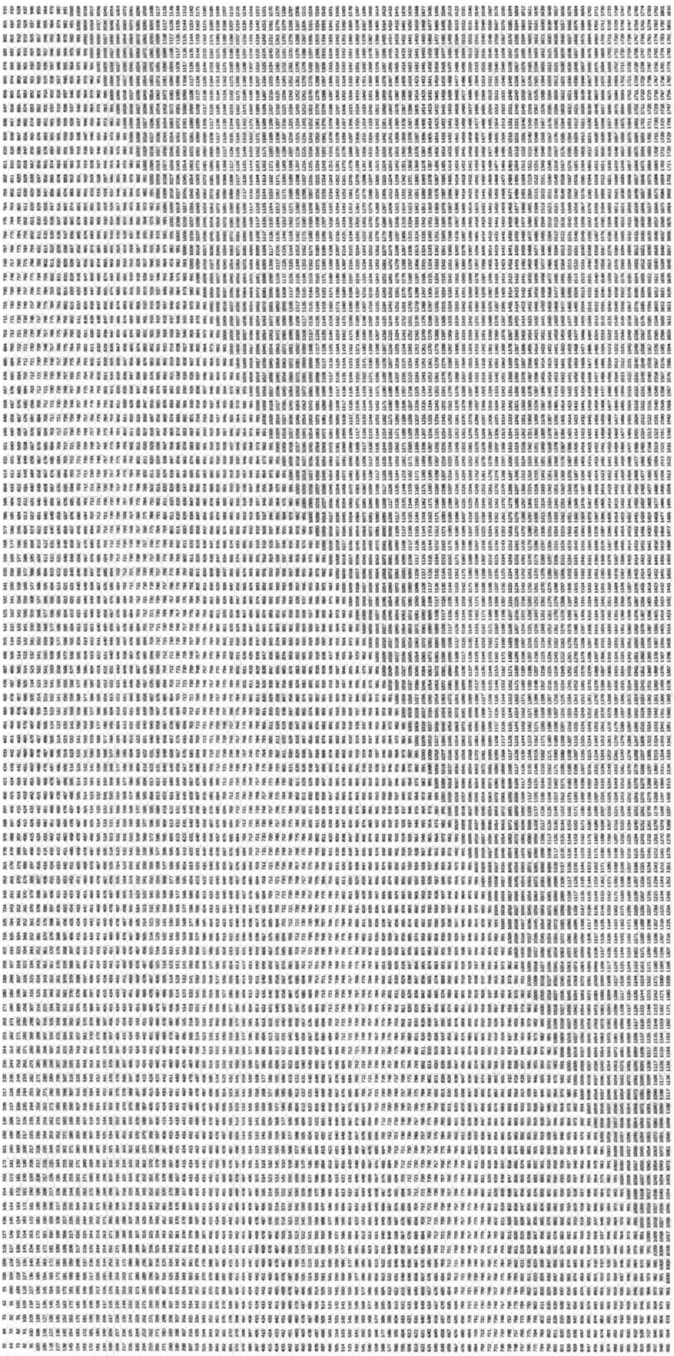

Figure 9.1 RAM—Ravana's Algorithmic Matrix.
(https://github.com/southpau79/ManusCrypt)

H (Xn) = 5767307d4246d3e609fbb864e84bcaf0829d8f48e524a5
961dc4146720821c8a3f0542ab28ca60c213f08ccffbb16f8c562c0
7c58fe098479898c1a93da07470 (Whirlpool)

The user password stored during the initial registration also has a hash value:

User password = st0nE@491
H (Xp) = 05af8cb1a7e3e75551d1fd8ab8f37e5608269f7df4e426b1
c2b6844c3e1874c8a6d8ec61519e0f170de31e6945f53368f63519f
9536a34f2c01d21aeae34341a
(Whirlpool)

So now we have,

H (Xu) = H (Xn) + H (Xp)
H (Xu) = c449e0524e9ebb36e81aa9d355c5a8ee23cc6bc4afaf9a0d6
7b7ec6fb8faeeebb59e5f5a8e93b0176a0cdb8fb8d101721b650b48e
d9724550acf387a3ee4ea4f (SHA3–512)

This final hash value is then validated via the CCF:
For ease of doing business here, let us take the value directly instead of the hash value as it would be very cumbersome to demonstrate the same in text.
In our example we have,

$X_n = X_{66} = 667$ so,

$667 \rightarrow 2{,}002 \rightarrow 1{,}001 \rightarrow 3{,}004 \rightarrow 1{,}502 \rightarrow 751 \rightarrow 2{,}254 \rightarrow 1{,}127 \rightarrow$
$\quad 3{,}382 \rightarrow 1{,}691 \rightarrow 5{,}074 \rightarrow 2{,}537 \rightarrow 7{,}612 \rightarrow 3{,}806 \rightarrow 1{,}903 \rightarrow$
$\quad 5{,}710 \rightarrow 2{,}855 \rightarrow 8{,}566 \rightarrow 4{,}283 \rightarrow 12{,}850 \rightarrow 6{,}425 \rightarrow 19{,}276 \rightarrow$
$\quad 9{,}638 \rightarrow 4{,}819 \rightarrow 14{,}458 \rightarrow 7{,}229 \rightarrow 21{,}688 \rightarrow 10{,}844 \rightarrow 5{,}422 \rightarrow$
$\quad 2{,}711 \rightarrow 8{,}134 \rightarrow 4{,}067 \rightarrow 12{,}202 \rightarrow 6{,}101 \rightarrow 18{,}304 \rightarrow 9{,}152 \rightarrow$
$\quad 4{,}576 \rightarrow 2{,}288 \rightarrow 1{,}144 \rightarrow 572 \rightarrow 286 \rightarrow$
$143 \rightarrow 430 \rightarrow 215 \rightarrow 646 \rightarrow 323 \rightarrow 970 \rightarrow 485 \rightarrow 1{,}456 \rightarrow 728 \rightarrow$
$\quad 364 \rightarrow 182 \rightarrow 91 \rightarrow 274 \rightarrow 137 \rightarrow 412 \rightarrow 206 \rightarrow 103 \rightarrow 310 \rightarrow$
$\quad 155 \rightarrow 466 \rightarrow 233 \rightarrow 700 \rightarrow 350 \rightarrow 175 \rightarrow 526 \rightarrow 263 \rightarrow 790 \rightarrow$
$\quad 395 \rightarrow 1{,}186 \rightarrow 593 \rightarrow 1{,}780 \rightarrow 890 \rightarrow 445 \rightarrow 1{,}336 \rightarrow 668 \rightarrow$
$\quad 334 \rightarrow 167 \rightarrow 502 \rightarrow 251 \rightarrow 754 \rightarrow 377 \rightarrow 1{,}132 \rightarrow 566 \rightarrow 283 \rightarrow$
$\quad 850 \rightarrow 425 \rightarrow 1{,}276 \rightarrow 638 \rightarrow 319 \rightarrow 958 \rightarrow 479 \rightarrow 1{,}438 \rightarrow 719$
$\quad \rightarrow 2{,}158 \rightarrow 1{,}079 \rightarrow 3{,}238 \rightarrow 1{,}619 \rightarrow 4{,}858 \rightarrow 2{,}429 \rightarrow 7{,}288$
$\quad \rightarrow 3{,}644 \rightarrow 1{,}822 \rightarrow 911 \rightarrow 2{,}734 \rightarrow 1{,}367 \rightarrow 4{,}102 \rightarrow 2{,}051 \rightarrow$
$\quad 6{,}154 \rightarrow 3{,}077 \rightarrow 9{,}232 \rightarrow 4{,}616 \rightarrow 2{,}308 \rightarrow 1{,}154 \rightarrow 577 \rightarrow$
$\quad 1{,}732 \rightarrow 866 \rightarrow 433 \rightarrow 1{,}300 \rightarrow 650 \rightarrow 325 \rightarrow 976 \rightarrow 488 \rightarrow 244$
$\quad \rightarrow 122 \rightarrow 61 \rightarrow 184 \rightarrow 92 \rightarrow 46 \rightarrow 23 \rightarrow 70 \rightarrow 35 \rightarrow 106 \rightarrow 53 \rightarrow$
$\quad 160 \rightarrow 80 \rightarrow 40 \rightarrow 20 \rightarrow 10 \rightarrow 5 \rightarrow 16 \rightarrow 8 \rightarrow 4 \rightarrow 2 \rightarrow 1$

In this manner a lot of critical attacks are rendered useless for, e.g., keylogging, privileged access, social engineering, eavesdropping, etc.

Please note that the explanation in this book has been oversimplified to convey the overall concept viz. anthropocentric information security. The real-world implementation has to be more complex involving several chunks of steps, stages, and processes.

Further, it is not practicable to discuss the detailed engineering involved for two reasons—

1. Explaining even one complete process in detail in a readable format would exceed the entire length of this book due to the complexity of the subject matter involved
2. Certain chunks pertain to be protected by IPR and patent laws, if not currently, then in the near future as and when the complete tool is implemented.

9.3 NOTE

RAM is just one example of IGF. There can be innumerable customized IGF tables and accordingly the user might receive different images each time for authentication, e.g., David and Goliath, Snow White and the Seven Dwarfs, etc.

Chapter 10

Architectural Appraisal

10.1 OVERVIEW OF SOLUTION

A humanistic design approach within the context of information security—that is what this book is all about. Let me reiterate that the proposed solution is just one of many and is not intended to replace or substitute the existing cryptography methods. In fact, it is supposed to act like an additional layer of security specifically meant for end-point security.

10.1.1 N-Tier Architecture

A three-tier software architecture is a popular architectural pattern that divides a software application into three distinct layers or tiers, each with specific responsibilities. In this scenario, we have a three-tier architecture comprising Common Lisp at the low level, Python as middleware, and Golang with React at the front end.

1. Low-Level Layer (Common Lisp)

- Common Lisp, a powerful and extensible programming language, serves as the low-level layer in this architecture.
- Common Lisp is well suited for tasks that require close interaction with hardware or low-level system operations.
- Responsibilities at this layer may include handling system-level operations, data processing, and interacting with databases or lower-level resources.
- Common Lisp is known for its efficiency, making it suitable for performance-critical tasks.

2. Middleware Layer (Python)

- Python, a versatile and high-level programming language, is used as the middleware layer.
- Python is known for its ease of use and extensive library support, making it a suitable choice for building middleware components.

- Responsibilities at this layer include business logic, data transformation, communication with the low-level layer (Common Lisp), and exposing APIs to the front-end layer.
- Python can handle tasks such as authentication, data validation, and communication with external services or databases.

3. Front-End Layer (Golang with React)

- The front-end layer is responsible for presenting the user interface to end users and interacting with them.
- Golang (or Go) is used for server-side logic in the front-end layer. Go is known for its performance and simplicity, making it a great choice for building web servers.
- React, a JavaScript library for building user interfaces, is used for the client side of the front end. React allows for the creation of interactive and responsive user interfaces.
- Golang handles tasks such as routing, API communication, and server-side rendering of React components.
- React handles the dynamic rendering of user interfaces, user interactions, and state management.

In summary, this three-tier software architecture leverages the strengths of each technology stack:

- Common Lisp at the low level for efficient, low-level operations.
- Python as middleware for business logic and communication between layers.
- Golang with React at the front end for high-performance, server-side logic and interactive user interfaces.

This architecture allows for modularity, scalability, and maintainability, as each layer has well-defined responsibilities, making it easier to develop, test, and maintain different parts of the application independently. Simplified high-level design architecture is presented for interested readers.

Please do note that the entire tool can be on chip, i.e., STONE (secure token on-chip network enumerator)—a physical key that is FIDO compliant. In the absence of a physical key, the same can be transformed into a serverless architecture accessed via a web API.

In this manner, multiple and simultaneous log-in attempts can be prevented without any manual intervention and even a privileged access cannot be leveraged to gain authentication.

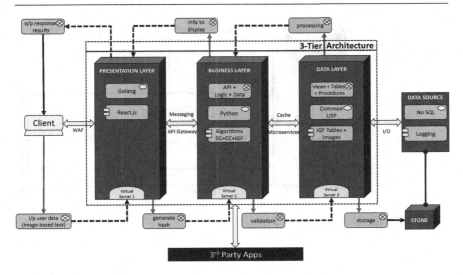

Figure 10.1 ManusCrypt Architecture.

10.2 UTILIZING EMERGING TECHNOLOGIES

As mentioned, STONE, i.e., a physical key can be utilized to make it more secure at the end point. Taking this further, another feature that can be added is the utilization of emerging technologies like blockchain and artificial intelligence.

Each log-in attempt / user authentication transaction can be stored over a private permissioned blockchain network where the authenticity of the transaction can be validated and stored for verification. Further, the logged data can be analyzed for patterns using various machine learning algorithms for further improvements.

A sample high-level design is provided in Figure 10.2, for those inquisitive readers who are interested. It can be a private / public permissioned blockchain as the case may be. The ordering peer, i.e., the user node (can be the client directly or STONE device), pushes the transactions into blocks over the network where the validating peer validates the blocks and the witness peer provides added assurance after validation. All the blocks containing all the transactions are replicated on the ledger and a copy of the ledger is available with each peer over the network in real time. All the peers communicate with each other over the "channel" as designated by the blockchain operator. This added layer provides complete security of the transaction, i.e., user authentication that cannot be replicated via conventional attacks by hackers.

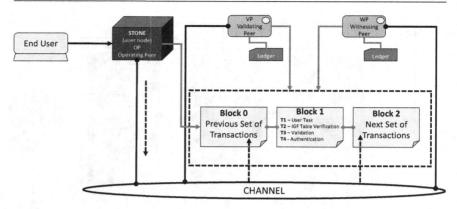

Figure 10.2 Blockchain for ManusCrypt.

Chapter 11

Paradigm Shift

11.1 FUTURE OF CRYPTOGRAPHY

In this age and times, there is a constant human dilemma that we are caught in. The journey from ancient ciphers to modern-day advanced cryptographic techniques has brought us into a multistoried sand castle. We can neither change the foundation nor can we strengthen the walls of sand. So, what do we do next?

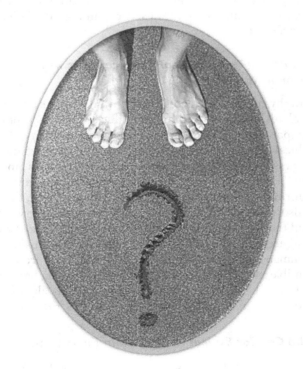

Figure 11.1 Human Dilemma.

DOI: 10.1201/9781003527220-12

11.1.1 Quantum Cryptography: A New Frontier

The future of cryptography holds exciting prospects, and one of the most promising frontiers is quantum cryptography. Quantum computing, a groundbreaking technology that leverages the principles of quantum mechanics, has the potential to revolutionize the field of cryptography.

Unlike classical computers that rely on bits to process data, quantum computers use quantum bits, or qubits, which can exist in multiple states simultaneously. This property allows quantum computers to perform complex calculations at an unprecedented speed, making traditional encryption methods vulnerable to quantum attacks.

Quantum cryptography offers a solution to this challenge by leveraging the principles of quantum mechanics to develop quantum-resistant encryption algorithms. Quantum key distribution (QKD) is a particularly noteworthy advancement in quantum cryptography, allowing two parties to share encryption keys securely through the quantum entanglement of particles.

While quantum cryptography holds great promise for enhancing data security, it is still in its infancy, and practical implementations face significant technological and engineering challenges. Researchers and technologists are actively exploring the possibilities of quantum cryptography, with the aim of ensuring data privacy and security in the face of quantum computing advancements.

11.1.1.1 Balancing Technological Advancements with Human Values

As cryptography continues to evolve, it is crucial to strike a balance between technological advancements and human values. While encryption technologies offer unparalleled protection for privacy and security, they also raise complex ethical dilemmas that demand thoughtful consideration.

As we witness the growth of artificial intelligence, big data, and the internet of things (IoT), encryption plays an even more critical role in safeguarding sensitive information and ensuring data integrity. However, this data-driven landscape also poses challenges, such as the potential for widespread surveillance and the monetization of personal data without user consent.

As we embrace technological advancements, we must remain vigilant about protecting human values, such as privacy, autonomy, and freedom of expression. Responsible encryption practices, transparency in data handling, and user-centric design can help ensure that technology remains aligned with human values, empowering individuals to maintain control over their digital lives.

11.1.1.2 The Call for Ethical Innovation in Encryption

The journey through the intricate world of modern cryptography has revealed the profound impact of encryption on humanity. From the ancient art of secret communication to the complex algorithms of today, cryptography has shaped the course of history and revolutionized how we interact, communicate, and perceive privacy.

As we stand at the precipice of a digital future, it is essential to reflect on the ethical and social implications of cryptographic technologies and policies. The future of cryptography is intertwined with the future of humanity, necessitating a careful and thoughtful approach to ensure that technology serves human values rather than stifles them.

In the future of cryptography, ethical considerations must be at the forefront of innovation. The growing interconnectivity of the digital world demands that technologists, policymakers, and society collaborate to develop encryption practices that prioritize user privacy and data protection.

11.1.1.3 Ethical Innovation in Encryption Involves

Inclusivity: Ensuring that encryption technologies are accessible and usable for all individuals, irrespective of their technological literacy or socioeconomic background.

Accountability: Holding technology companies and governments accountable for their data practices, encryption implementations, and user privacy.

User Empowerment: Empowering users with tools and knowledge to make informed decisions about their data and privacy.

Public Discourse: Encouraging open and transparent discussions about the ethical implications of cryptography, involving stakeholders from diverse backgrounds.

Global Cooperation: Fostering international cooperation and collaboration to address encryption challenges and promote global data privacy standards.

11.1.1.4 Privacy and Personal Agency

Privacy is a cornerstone of human dignity, providing individuals with the freedom to express themselves, explore ideas, and form intimate relationships. Ethical cryptographic practices should prioritize user privacy, empowering individuals with personal agency over their data and digital identities.

As governments and corporations wield increasing power in the digital realm, the responsible use of encryption becomes an essential bulwark against potential abuses of power. Privacy-enhancing technologies and robust encryption systems will be vital in preserving the essence of humanity—the ability to be ourselves without fear of surveillance or manipulation.

11.1.1.5 Empowering Digital Citizenship

Digital literacy and cyber awareness are essential facets of modern citizenship. As we move towards an increasingly interconnected world, ethical cryptographic practices should prioritize digital inclusion and accessibility.

Empowering individuals with knowledge about encryption and responsible data practices ensures that they can navigate the digital landscape safely and responsibly. This sense of digital agency will be critical in fostering a society where technology serves human interests rather than subjugates them.

11.1.1.6 The Role of Technology Companies

Technology companies play a pivotal role in shaping the future of cryptography and humanity. As guardians of user data, they bear the responsibility of protecting individual privacy and upholding ethical data practices.

Responsible data management, transparency, and user-centric design will be key in earning and maintaining user trust. By prioritizing user privacy over profit, technology companies can demonstrate a commitment to human values, fostering a digital ecosystem that respects individual rights and fosters trust.

11.1.1.7 Innovative Solutions and Public Policy

The future of cryptography hinges on the development of innovative solutions that navigate the ethical tightrope of security and human values. Researchers and technologists must continue exploring cutting-edge cryptographic techniques that prioritize privacy and accountability.

Public policy must also keep pace with technological advancements, promoting legislation that strikes a harmonious balance between security imperatives and individual liberties. Multilateral collaboration among governments, technology companies, and civil society will be essential in crafting policies that transcend national borders and uphold human rights in the digital age.

11.1.1.8 The Ethical Imperative

Above all, the future of cryptography must be driven by an ethical imperative—a commitment to preserving human values, dignity, and freedom. Encryption should empower individuals, foster trust, and promote digital citizenship. It should safeguard democracy, protect human rights, and foster inclusivity in the digital realm.

Embracing this ethical imperative requires continuous reflection, dialogue, and collective action. As we shape the future of cryptography and humanity, we must approach this endeavor with a deep sense of responsibility and a commitment to promoting technology that enhances human flourishing.

In conclusion, the world of modern cryptography is a complex tapestry, woven from ancient secrets to cutting-edge algorithms. Its impact on humanity is profound and multifaceted, shaping our interactions, perceptions, and vulnerabilities.

As we step into the future, let us approach the cryptographic landscape with ethical wisdom and a commitment to human values. Through responsible data practices, transparency, and inclusive policies, we can build a future where technology empowers individuals, upholds privacy, and serves the greater good of humanity.

The journey of cryptography and its interaction with humanity is ongoing. In the ever-evolving digital landscape, let us continue to navigate with ethical mindfulness, striving to create a world where technology and humanity coexist in harmony—a world that cherishes privacy, respects individual rights, and celebrates the human spirit.

The future of cryptography is marked by technological advancements, quantum computing, and the proliferation of data-driven technologies. As we venture into this new era, it is essential to keep human values and ethics at the core of our approach to encryption.

Quantum cryptography presents an exciting frontier that holds the potential to enhance data security in the face of evolving threats. However, striking the right balance between technology and human values is critical to ensure that encryption continues to serve as a pillar of privacy, autonomy, and individual freedoms.

By embracing ethical innovation, promoting transparency, and fostering collaboration, we can shape a future where cryptography empowers individuals, strengthens societies, and advances the greater good in our ever-evolving digital landscape.

11.2 EMBRACING THE HUMAN ELEMENT

11.2.1 A Human-Centric Approach to Encryption

As technology continues to shape the modern world, it is essential to center cryptography around the human element. A human-centric approach to encryption acknowledges that technology should serve and empower individuals, rather than control or surveil them.

The human element encompasses various aspects, including individual rights, privacy, autonomy, and the right to make informed decisions about personal data. Encryption should be designed to respect and protect these aspects, ensuring that individuals can interact with technology and digital platforms with confidence and without fear of undue intrusion.

11.2.2 Empowering Individuals in Digital Security

Empowering individuals in digital security is at the core of a human-centric approach to encryption. This involves providing accessible tools, resources, and knowledge that enable individuals to take control of their digital lives and protect their sensitive information.

Digital literacy and cybersecurity awareness play a crucial role in empowering individuals. Education on best practices for data protection, password hygiene, and recognizing potential cyber threats can help individuals navigate the digital landscape with confidence.

Technology companies and encryption providers can contribute to empowerment by offering user-friendly interfaces, clear privacy policies, and transparent data practices. By placing the user at the center of their design and decision-making processes, these entities can create encryption solutions that prioritize usability, accessibility, and user agency.

11.2.3 Privacy by Design: A Step Towards Reconciliation

Privacy by design is a principle that advocates for the integration of privacy considerations into the design and development of technologies from the outset. Applying this principle to encryption solutions ensures that privacy and data protection are embedded into the very fabric of digital platforms.

By adopting a privacy-by-design approach, encryption solutions can reconcile the apparent tensions between security imperatives and individual rights. Privacy by design emphasizes the importance of proactive measures to protect data and privacy, rather than relying on afterthoughts or reactive solutions.

11.2.4 Implementing Privacy by Design Involves

Data Minimization: Collecting only the data necessary for the intended purpose and ensuring data is anonymized or pseudonymized whenever possible.

Access Control: Limiting access to sensitive information to authorized entities and ensuring encryption mechanisms protect data at rest and in transit.

Transparent Data Practices: Being transparent with users about data collection, processing, and sharing, providing clear privacy policies and user consent mechanisms.

User Empowerment: Empowering users with granular control over their data and privacy settings, allowing them to make informed decisions about how their information is used.

In this penultimate chapter of our exploration into the world of cryptography and its impact on humanity, we embrace the concept of ethical cryptography as a guiding principle for shaping a harmonious future. Ethical cryptography calls for a thoughtful and responsible approach to the development, deployment, and regulation of cryptographic technologies, with a focus on upholding human values, privacy, and individual rights.

11.2.5 Empowering Individual Privacy and Autonomy

At the core of ethical cryptography lies the belief that individuals should have control over their personal data and digital identities. Encryption should serve as a tool to empower privacy, giving people the confidence to express themselves freely without fear of surveillance or intrusion.

Technology companies must prioritize privacy by design, building encryption systems that prioritize user agency and data protection. By putting privacy at the forefront of their products and services, companies can forge a path towards a future where individuals are in control of their digital lives.

11.2.6 Resisting Surveillance Overreach

Ethical cryptography resists the temptation of surveillance overreach, where governments and entities exploit technology to engage in mass surveillance and erode civil liberties. Balancing legitimate national security concerns with the preservation of individual rights requires a nuanced approach to policy-making.

Multilateral cooperation and transparent dialogue between governments, tech companies, and civil society are essential to crafting encryption policies that protect public safety without sacrificing privacy. Ethical cryptographic policies should aim to strike a delicate balance between security imperatives and human rights, ensuring that technology enhances rather than diminishes the fabric of democratic societies.

11.2.7 Promoting Digital Literacy and Inclusivity

A harmonious future requires a digitally literate populace that can navigate the complexities of modern cryptography responsibly. Ethical cryptographic practices involve investing in educational initiatives to empower individuals with the knowledge and skills to protect themselves in the digital landscape.

Promoting digital inclusivity is equally crucial. Bridging the digital divide and ensuring accessibility to secure communication tools will empower marginalized communities to participate fully in the digital realm without compromising their privacy or safety.

11.2.8 Responsible Innovation and Collaboration

In the pursuit of a harmonious future, responsible innovation and collaboration are paramount. Researchers, technologists, and policymakers must work hand in hand to develop cryptographic solutions that prioritize privacy, transparency, and accountability.

The spirit of collaboration should extend beyond national borders, transcending geopolitical boundaries to address global challenges. In a world interconnected by digital networks, international cooperation is crucial in formulating ethical cryptographic policies that uphold human rights and democratic values.

11.2.9 A Moral Compass for Technology Companies

Technology companies wield immense power and influence in the digital age. Ethical cryptography demands that they act as responsible stewards of user data, prioritizing privacy and transparency in their operations.

By adhering to ethical data practices, earning and maintaining user trust, and being accountable for the impact of their products, technology companies can serve as a moral compass in the digital landscape. This commitment to human values will pave the way for a future where technology aligns with the best interests of humanity.

Embracing the human element in cryptography is vital as technology continues to shape our digital lives. A human-centric approach to encryption prioritizes individual rights, privacy, and empowerment, ensuring that technology serves humanity rather than controlling it.

By empowering individuals in digital security through education, accessible tools, and user-centric design, we can create a digital landscape where users feel in control of their data and interactions. Privacy by design plays a key role in reconciling the apparent conflicts between security and individual rights, providing a foundation for encryption solutions that respect human values and ethical principles.

As we move forward into the future of cryptography, let us embrace the human element as the guiding principle in our pursuit of privacy, security, and digital empowerment. By doing so, we can create a more inclusive and equitable digital world where technology fosters human potential and serves the greater good of humanity.

11.3 A HARMONIOUS SYNTHESIS

As we conclude our journey through the world of cryptography and its intricate relationship with humanity, we find ourselves at a crossroads—a juncture where ethical cryptography illuminates the path forward.

In the tapestry of human progress, cryptography has woven threads of secrecy, security, and revelation. Its impact on society has been profound, shaping our lives and interactions in ways both visible and unseen.

In forging a harmonious future, we must embrace the ethical imperative—navigating the digital landscape with a deep sense of responsibility and a commitment to human values. Privacy, inclusivity, transparency, and user agency must guide our endeavors as we shape cryptographic technologies and policies.

The future of cryptography is not predetermined; it is a collective creation—an intricate synthesis of technology and humanity. By harnessing the power of ethical cryptography, we can weave a fabric that embraces privacy, empowers individuals, and elevates human dignity.

As we venture forth, let us carry with us the wisdom gained from our exploration—a wisdom that invites us to envision a future where technology serves the greater good of humanity, harmoniously coexisting with the essence of who we are. Together, we can shape a world where ethical cryptography becomes the foundation of a digital landscape that celebrates our diversity, respects our rights, and empowers us to thrive in a world of endless possibilities.

11.3.1 Embracing the Shadows

Cryptography, like shadows cast by the sun, is an inherent part of our digital world, subtly influencing our lives and interactions. As we traverse the landscape of modern technology, it is essential to approach cryptography with a balanced vision that embraces both its benefits and challenges.

11.3.2 A Balanced Vision: Coexisting with Cryptography

Cryptographic technologies have transformed the way we communicate, transact, and interact in the digital realm. From protecting sensitive information to enabling secure online transactions, cryptography has become a pillar of modern data security.

However, this journey is not without its shadows. The clash between security imperatives and individual rights, the tension between privacy and surveillance, and the ethical dilemmas surrounding encryption have forced us to grapple with complex and multifaceted challenges.

Embracing a balanced vision means recognizing that cryptography is not a panacea for all digital problems. It is a powerful tool that demands responsible and ethical implementation to safeguard individual liberties while fulfilling societal needs.

11.3.3 The Path towards a Human-Centered Cryptography

A human-centered approach to cryptography lies at the heart of embracing the shadows. By prioritizing the human element—privacy, autonomy, empowerment, and informed consent—we can shape encryption solutions that respect human dignity and uphold ethical values.

Empowering individuals in digital security through education, accessible tools, and transparent data practices is crucial for fostering a sense of agency and control over personal data. By placing individuals at the center of encryption design and decision-making, we can navigate the digital landscape with confidence, knowing that technology serves our best interests.

11.3.4 Securing the Future While Respecting the Essence of Humanity

As we secure the future of cryptography, we must do so while respecting the essence of humanity. Encryption should not become an instrument of control or surveillance, but a shield that protects individual freedoms, enables open communication, and fosters societal progress.

This journey requires collaboration, dialogue, and a commitment to shared principles. It is a path that demands transparency, accountability, and a continuous examination of the ethical implications of encryption.

By embracing the shadows cast by cryptography, we acknowledge the complexities of the digital age and the challenges it presents. With a balanced vision and a human-centered approach, we can navigate these shadows with wisdom and integrity, forging a future where technology serves humanity while upholding the values of privacy, security, and human dignity.

As we continue on this path, let us remember that the shadows are not to be feared but understood. By embracing them, we can illuminate the way forward, ensuring that cryptography remains a force for good in our ever-changing world. With responsible encryption practices, empathy, and a commitment to the greater good, we can shape a digital future that empowers individuals, strengthens societies, and respects the essence of humanity.

Chapter 12

Technical Notes

This chapter has been included especially for the uninitiated. In case you do not belong to the IT industry or even if you do but have no idea about cryptography and encryption, you can quickly grasp the basics from here. Though the subject matter presented in this book has far-reaching implications, the business use-case scenario presented herein has been narrowed down to "user authentication".

So, let's begin with the basics.

12.1 CRYPTOGRAPHY AND ITS TYPES

Cryptography is the science and art of securing communication and data by transforming plaintext (readable) information into ciphertext (unreadable) through various mathematical algorithms and techniques. There are several types of cryptography, each serving specific purposes and applications. Let's explore some of the major types of cryptography:

12.1.1 Symmetric Key Cryptography

Symmetric key cryptography, also known as secret-key cryptography, involves the use of a single secret key for both encryption and decryption of data. The key must be kept secret between the sender and receiver. The main advantage of symmetric encryption is its efficiency, making it suitable for encrypting large amounts of data.

How it works

Encryption: The plaintext is combined with the secret key using a cryptographic algorithm to produce ciphertext.

Decryption: The recipient uses the same secret key and algorithm to convert the ciphertext back into plaintext.

The challenge with symmetric cryptography is securely exchanging the secret key between parties, as it needs to be kept secret from potential attackers.

12.1.2 Asymmetric Key Cryptography (Public-Key Cryptography)

Asymmetric key cryptography utilizes a pair of keys, a public key, and a private key. These keys are mathematically related but cannot be derived from one another. The public key is openly distributed, while the private key is kept secret. This type of cryptography offers a solution to the key exchange problem faced by symmetric key cryptography.

How it works

Encryption: The sender uses the recipient's public key to encrypt the message into ciphertext.

Decryption: Only the recipient, possessing the corresponding private key, can decrypt the ciphertext and retrieve the original plaintext.

Asymmetric cryptography is computationally more intensive than symmetric cryptography but provides better security and key management.

12.1.3 Hash Functions

Hash functions are one-way mathematical algorithms that take an input (plaintext) and produce a fixed-size string of characters called a hash value or digest. The key features of hash functions are that they are irreversible and produce a unique hash for each unique input. They are widely used in digital signatures and ensuring data integrity.

How it works

Data Integrity: A sender computes the hash value of the data and sends both the data and the hash to the recipient. The recipient recomputes the hash of the received data and compares it with the received hash. If they match, the data remains unchanged.

12.1.4 Message Authentication Codes (MACs)

MACs are a type of symmetric cryptographic technique used to verify the integrity and authenticity of a message. A MAC is generated using a secret key, ensuring that only parties with access to the secret key can verify the MAC's validity.

How it works

Calculation: The sender combines the message with the secret key to produce the MAC.

Verification: The recipient performs the same calculation using the received message and the shared secret key. If the calculated MAC matches the received MAC, the message's integrity and authenticity are verified.

12.1.5 Digital Signatures

Digital signatures are a crucial component of asymmetric cryptography used to verify the authenticity and integrity of digital messages or documents. They are created using the sender's private key and can be verified using the corresponding public key.

How it works

Signature Generation: The sender applies a cryptographic algorithm to the message and their private key, generating a unique digital signature.

Signature Verification: The recipient uses the sender's public key and the received message to verify the digital signature's authenticity and integrity.

These are some of the major types of cryptography, each with its unique strengths and applications in securing data, ensuring privacy, and verifying the authenticity and integrity of digital communication. Cryptography plays a critical role in safeguarding sensitive information and maintaining secure communication in the digital age.

12.2 USES OF CRYPTOGRAPHY

Cryptography, the practice of secure communication in the presence of adversaries, has a wide range of uses across various domains. Here are some common applications of cryptography:

Confidentiality: Cryptography can be used to ensure confidentiality by encrypting data. Encrypted data can only be deciphered by authorized parties with the corresponding decryption key. This application is crucial for protecting sensitive information during transmission or storage.

Data Integrity: Cryptographic techniques such as hashing and digital signatures are used to ensure data integrity. Hash functions generate unique hash values for data, allowing detection of any modifications or tampering. Digital signatures provide a way to verify the authenticity and integrity of digital documents.

Authentication: Cryptography is employed in authentication processes to verify the identity of users or entities. Techniques like digital certificates, public-key infrastructure (PKI), and secure key exchange protocols enable secure authentication, preventing impersonation and unauthorized access.

Non-Repudiation: Cryptographic methods like digital signatures provide non-repudiation, ensuring that a sender cannot deny sending a message or performing a transaction. Digital signatures provide evidence of the origin and integrity of a message, making them legally enforceable in certain contexts.

Secure Communication: Cryptography plays a crucial role in securing communication channels. Transport Layer Security (TLS) and Secure Sockets Layer (SSL) protocols use cryptographic algorithms to encrypt data exchanged between web servers and browsers, protecting against eavesdropping and tampering.

Password Storage: Cryptographic techniques are employed to securely store passwords. Rather than storing passwords in plain text, they are usually hashed and salted to protect against unauthorized access in case of a data breach.

Virtual Private Networks (VPNs): Cryptography is integral to VPNs, which provide secure and private communication over public networks. VPNs encrypt network traffic, ensuring confidentiality and protecting sensitive data from unauthorized access.

Secure Transactions: Cryptography is utilized in securing financial transactions, such as online banking and e-commerce. Technologies like Secure Electronic Transactions (SET) and Secure Sockets Layer (SSL) ensure the confidentiality and integrity of payment information during transmission.

Digital Rights Management (DRM): Cryptography is employed in DRM systems to protect copyrighted digital content from unauthorized access, distribution, and copying. Encryption techniques ensure that only authorized users can access and use the protected content.

Secure Storage: Cryptographic algorithms are used to encrypt data stored on devices or in databases. This protects sensitive information from unauthorized access in case of physical theft or data breaches.

These are just a few examples of the many uses of cryptography. Cryptographic techniques are essential for ensuring the security, privacy, and integrity of digital communication, transactions, and data in various fields, including cybersecurity, finance, healthcare, government, and more.

12.3 USER AUTHENTICATION PROCESS

When you enter your log-in ID and password on a website, several processes occur behind the scenes to authenticate your credentials and grant you access to the website. Here's a general overview of what happens:

User Input: You enter your log-in ID (username, email, or any identifier) and password into the log-in form on the website.

Data Transmission: When you click the "Submit" button, your web browser sends an HTTP POST request to the website's server, containing the log-in credentials you entered. The data is typically sent over a secure connection using HTTPS to ensure encryption.

Server-Side Processing: The website's server receives the request and initiates the log-in authentication process. The server retrieves the stored user account information from its database based on the provided log-in ID.

Password Hashing: To protect user passwords, most websites do not store them in plain text. Instead, they use a process called hashing. The server takes the password you entered, applies a one-way mathematical algorithm (hash function) to it, and converts it into a fixed-length string of characters. The resulting hash is then compared to the stored hash value associated with your account.

Hash Comparison: The server compares the hashed password from the database with the newly generated hash of the entered password. If the two hashes match, it indicates that the passwords are the same, and the authentication process proceeds. Otherwise, if the hashes do not match, it means the entered password is incorrect.

Session Creation: If the password matches, the server generates a unique session identifier or token, which is associated with your log-in session. This session identifier is stored on the server and sent back to your browser as a response to the log-in request.

Cookie Creation: To maintain the session, the server also sends a small text file called a cookie to your browser. This cookie contains the session identifier, which is stored on your computer.

Access Granted: Your browser receives the session identifier and the cookie, and it stores the cookie locally. It then includes the cookie in subsequent requests to the website, allowing the server to recognize and identify your ongoing session.

Website Interaction: With the session established, you are now authenticated and granted access to the website's protected resources. You can navigate through the site and perform actions as an authenticated user.

Session Management: The server keeps track of your session throughout your interaction with the website. It may store session-related information, such as your preferences, in a database or cache to personalize your experience.

It's important to note that different websites may have variations in their authentication processes, but the general concepts of hashing passwords, creating sessions, and using cookies for session management are widely used. Additionally, websites may employ additional security measures like multi-factor authentication (MFA) to further enhance the log-in process's security.

12.4 HACKING A USER ACCOUNT

There are several ways in which your account can be hacked over the internet. Here are some common methods employed by attackers:

Brute-Force Attacks: Attackers use automated tools to systematically guess your log-in credentials by trying numerous combinations of usernames and passwords until they find the correct ones. Weak or easily guessable passwords make it easier for attackers to succeed in these attacks.

Phishing: Phishing is a technique where attackers create fake websites or emails that mimic legitimate ones to trick users into revealing their log-in credentials. They may send you an email with a link to a fake log-in page that looks identical to the real one, and when you enter your credentials, they are captured by the attacker.

Credential Reuse: If you use the same username and password combination across multiple websites, a data breach on one site can lead to the compromise of your other accounts. Attackers often target less secure websites, obtain user credentials, and then try those credentials on popular sites.

Malware: Malicious software, such as keyloggers or password stealers, can be unknowingly installed on your device through infected email attachments, downloads, or malicious websites. These programs record your keystrokes or capture log-in information from your browser, providing attackers with your account credentials.

Man-in-the-Middle (MitM) Attacks: In this attack, an attacker intercepts the communication between your device and the website you're accessing. By doing so, they can eavesdrop on your log-in credentials or modify the data exchanged between you and the website.

Session Hijacking: Attackers may attempt to steal your session cookies, which are used to authenticate your session with a website. If they can obtain your session cookie, they can impersonate you and gain unauthorized access to your account.

Account Enumeration: Attackers may exploit weaknesses in a website's authentication mechanism to determine valid usernames or email addresses. By discovering valid accounts, they can then focus their efforts on compromising those accounts through other means.

Social Engineering: Attackers may manipulate or deceive individuals to extract their log-in credentials. This can involve tactics like impersonating customer support, requesting personal information under false pretenses, or tricking users into revealing their passwords through phone calls or messages.

Protecting yourself from these risks involves practicing good security habits:

- Use strong and unique passwords for each of your online accounts.
- Enable multifactor authentication (MFA) whenever possible.
- Be cautious of suspicious emails, links, and attachments.
- Regularly update your software and use reputable security software to detect and remove malware.
- Only enter log-in credentials on secure and legitimate websites.
- Avoid using public Wi-Fi networks for sensitive activities without a reliable VPN (virtual private network).
- Stay informed about common hacking techniques and security best practices.

By being vigilant and adopting these measures, you can significantly reduce the risk of your accounts being hacked.

12.5 USER ACCOUNT COMPROMISES

The number of user account compromises can vary significantly depending on various factors, including the level of cybersecurity awareness, the adoption of security measures, and the number of data breaches reported. It's important to note that cybersecurity incidents and user account compromises can vary significantly from year to year and depend on global trends in cybercrime and security measures.

Cyberattacks can take various forms, each targeting different vulnerabilities in systems and human behavior. Here are some common methods and modes of cyberattacks that can compromise user accounts:

Data Breaches and Hacks: Major data breaches and cyberattacks have exposed billions of user account credentials, including usernames, passwords, and personal information. Attackers exploit vulnerabilities in systems to gain unauthorized access to databases containing user data.

Weak Passwords and Password Reuse: Users often use weak passwords or reuse the same password across multiple accounts, making it easier for attackers to compromise multiple accounts if one password is leaked.

Keyloggers: Malicious software, such as keyloggers, can record user keystrokes, allowing attackers to capture log-in credentials and other sensitive information.

Credential Stuffing: Cybercriminals use automated tools to try stolen username and password combinations across multiple websites to gain unauthorized access to user accounts.

Insider Threats: Attacks from within an organization by disgruntled employees or individuals with authorized access can also lead to account compromises.

Phishing Attacks: Phishing is a type of social engineering attack where attackers create deceptive emails, messages, or websites to trick users into revealing sensitive information, such as log-in credentials, credit card numbers, or personal details. Phishing attacks often mimic legitimate sources to deceive users.

Brute-Force Attacks: Attackers attempt to gain unauthorized access to user accounts by trying all possible combinations of usernames and passwords until they find the correct one. Brute force attacks are often used against weak or easily guessable passwords.

Man-in-the-Middle (MITM) Attacks: In a MITM attack, the attacker intercepts and relays communication between two parties, often altering the data exchanged. This allows attackers to capture log-in credentials and other sensitive information.

Session Hijacking: Attackers can steal a user's session cookies or tokens to impersonate the user and gain unauthorized access to their accounts without needing their actual log-in credentials.

Zero-Day Exploits: Zero-day exploits target vulnerabilities in software that are unknown to the software vendor or have not yet been patched. Attackers exploit these vulnerabilities to gain unauthorized access to user accounts or systems.

Malware Attacks: Malicious software, such as viruses, worms, and Trojans, can be used to gain access to user accounts, steal information, or enable other types of cyberattacks.

Pharming: In pharming attacks, attackers redirect users to fraudulent websites without their knowledge, even if the user types the correct website address in the browser. These fraudulent websites can be used to steal log-in credentials and other sensitive information.

Watering Hole Attacks: In a watering hole attack, attackers compromise a legitimate website that is frequently visited by the target audience. When users visit the compromised website, they may unknowingly download malware or be redirected to malicious sites.

Social Engineering: Social engineering attacks manipulate users into revealing sensitive information by exploiting their trust, curiosity, fear, or desire to help others. These attacks can occur over the phone, through emails, or in person.

To protect against these types of cyberattacks, users and organizations should adopt strong security practices, such as using unique and strong passwords, enabling multifactor authentication, keeping software up to date, being cautious with unsolicited emails and messages, and educating users about potential threats and best security practices.

12.6 CRYPTOGRAPHY AND AUTHENTICATION

Cryptography plays a crucial role in authentication processes by ensuring secure and reliable identification of users or entities. Here's how cryptography is used in authentication:

Password Encryption: When a user creates an account or sets a password, the password is typically encrypted using a cryptographic hash function. The hash function converts the password into a fixed-length string of characters, which is stored in the system's database instead of the actual password. This way, even if the database is compromised, the passwords remain protected.

Password Verification: When a user attempts to log in, the entered password is encrypted using the same hash function, and the resulting hash is compared with the stored hash in the database. If the hashes match, it indicates that the entered password is correct, and the user is granted access. This process ensures that the password remains undisclosed throughout the authentication process.

Challenge–Response Authentication: Cryptography is used in challenge–response protocols, where a server challenges a client to prove its identity. The server sends a unique challenge to the client, and the client must compute a cryptographic response based on the challenge and its secret key. The server verifies the response to authenticate the client's identity.

Public-Key Infrastructure (PKI): PKI is a system that uses asymmetric cryptography, involving the use of public- and private-key pairs. In authentication, a user's public-key is typically stored in a digital certificate issued by a trusted certificate authority (CA). When a user presents the certificate to a server, the server can verify the authenticity of the certificate and the associated public-key to authenticate the user.

Digital Signatures: Digital signatures are used to authenticate the integrity and origin of digital documents or messages. A digital signature is created using the signer's private key and can be verified using the corresponding public-key. By verifying the digital signature, the recipient can ensure that the message or document has not been tampered with and originated from the expected sender.

Two-Factor Authentication (2FA): Cryptography is employed in 2FA systems to provide an additional layer of security. One common approach is using a time-based one-time password (TOTP) algorithm, where a secret key is shared between the server and the user's device. The device generates a unique password that changes every few seconds, based on the shared secret and the current time. The server verifies the entered password against its own calculation to authenticate the user.

Secure Key Exchange: Cryptography is used in secure key exchange protocols like Diffie–Hellman or Elliptic Curve Diffie–Hellman (ECDH). These protocols allow two parties to establish a shared secret key over an insecure channel without revealing the key to eavesdroppers. The shared secret key can then be used for subsequent cryptographic operations, such as encryption and authentication.

By leveraging cryptographic techniques in authentication, organizations can ensure the confidentiality, integrity, and authenticity of user identities, protecting against unauthorized access and impersonation.

12.7 CRYPTOGRAPHY AND CRA

Challenge–response authentication is a cryptographic protocol used to verify the identity of a client or user by employing a challenge and response mechanism. It ensures that the client possesses a secret key without revealing the key itself during the authentication process. Here's a step-by-step description of how cryptography is involved in challenge–response authentication:

12.7.1 Setup

The server and client each have a unique secret key, usually generated using a secure random number generator.

Both the server and client have access to a cryptographic hash function, denoted as $H()$.

12.7.2 Challenge Phase

a. Server:
   The server generates a random challenge, represented as a value C.
   The challenge can be any random data, such as a nonce or a sequence of bits.
   The server sends the challenge C to the client.
b. Client:
   Upon receiving the challenge C, the client uses its secret key, denoted as K, to compute a response value R.

The client calculates the response using a cryptographic function, denoted as F():

$$R = F(K, C)$$

F() can be any suitable cryptographic function, such as a hash function or a symmetric encryption algorithm.

F() takes the secret key K and the challenge C as inputs and produces the response value R.

12.7.3 Response Phase

a. Client:
   The client sends the response value R to the server.
b. Server:
   Upon receiving the response R, the server uses the client's secret key K to compute the expected response value, denoted as R'.

The server performs the same calculation as the client:

$$R' = F(K, C)$$

Verification:

The server compares the received response R with the expected response R'.
If R matches R', the server accepts the client's identity as valid.
If R does not match R', the server rejects the client's identity.

In challenge–response authentication, the cryptographic function F() serves as the core mechanism that ensures the secrecy of the key and the authenticity of the response. The specific cryptographic function employed can vary, depending on the security requirements and the desired properties of the protocol.

The strength of challenge–response authentication lies in the assumption that only the legitimate client possesses the secret key K. Without knowing K, an attacker cannot generate the correct response R' to match the challenge C, making it difficult to impersonate the client.

It's important to note that the secure generation and management of secret keys, as well as the choice of a suitable cryptographic function, are critical aspects of implementing challenge–response authentication securely. Additionally, the protocol may need additional security measures, such as protecting the transmission of the challenge and response using encryption or secure channels, to further enhance its overall security.

Detailed technical review of how cryptography works in case of a challenge–response authentication process:

Challenge–response authentication is a cryptographic protocol used to verify the identity of a user or entity before granting access to a system or service. It is commonly used in various authentication scenarios, such as remote log-in, online banking, and secure communication. The process involves a challenge (random value) presented by the verifier to the user, who responds with the correct response based on their secret credentials (password or private key). Let's take a look at a detailed technical review of how cryptography works in a challenge–response authentication process:

12.7.4 Initialization

The user and the verifier must agree on the cryptographic algorithms and parameters they will use during the authentication process. This includes choosing a secure hash function, encryption algorithm, and key lengths.

12.7.5 User Registration

Before the authentication process, the user must register with the verifier. During registration, the user provides their identity (username), and a secret credential (e.g., password or private key) is generated. The verifier stores this secret credential securely, usually in hashed or encrypted form, to prevent unauthorized access to it.

12.7.6 The Challenge–Response Process

When the user attempts to authenticate with the system, the challenge–response process begins:

a. The verifier sends a challenge to the user. This challenge is a random value or a nonce generated by the verifier for this specific authentication attempt.
b. The user receives the challenge and computes the response using their secret credential and a cryptographic algorithm.

12.7.7 Response Calculation

The specific response calculation process depends on whether symmetric key cryptography or asymmetric key cryptography is used:

a. Symmetric Key Challenge–Response:
   If symmetric key cryptography is used, both the verifier and user share a secret key (previously established during registration).
   The user takes the challenge (nonce) and their secret key to compute the response.

For example, the user may compute the response as the cryptographic hash of the concatenation of the challenge and their secret key: response = hash(challenge ‖ secret_key).

    b. Asymmetric Key Challenge–Response:

        If asymmetric key cryptography is used, the user possesses a private key (secret key) and a corresponding public-key. The public-key is known to the verifier.

        The user uses their private key to sign the challenge, producing the response.

        The verifier will use the public-key to verify the response's authenticity.

12.7.8 Response Submission and Verification

The user sends the computed response back to the verifier.

The verifier then performs its own calculation (using the same cryptographic algorithm and shared secret key or public-key) to verify the correctness of the response.

If the response matches the expected value, the verifier confirms the user's identity and grants access to the system or service. Otherwise, access is denied.

12.7.9 Key Points

Challenge–response authentication ensures that even if an attacker intercepts the challenge and response, they cannot use it for future authentication attempts. The challenge is typically unique for each authentication session, and the response depends on the challenge and the user's secret credential.

The cryptographic algorithms and key management are crucial for the security of the challenge–response authentication process. Using strong cryptographic algorithms and secure key generation and storage practices are essential to prevent attacks like brute-force or replay attacks.

Overall, challenge–response authentication, when combined with proper cryptographic techniques, provides a secure and reliable method to verify the identity of users and entities in various applications and systems.

12.8 HACKING CRA

In the challenge–response authentication process, the main goal of an attacker is to gain privileged access by impersonating the legitimate client or user. While the challenge–response mechanism itself is designed to be secure, there are potential vulnerabilities that attackers may exploit to achieve privileged access. Here are some ways hackers can attempt to gain privileged access in the challenge–response authentication process:

Brute-Force Attacks: Attackers may try to guess or systematically enumerate possible secret keys in order to find the correct one. If the secret key used by the legitimate client is weak or easily guessable, such as a common password or a short key length, it becomes easier for attackers to perform a successful brute-force attack.

Man-in-the-Middle (MitM) Attacks: Attackers can intercept the communication between the client and the server during the challenge–response process. By positioning themselves as intermediaries, they can capture the challenge from the server, pass it to the client, capture the response from the client, and pass it to the server. The attacker can then proceed to authenticate themselves using the captured response, effectively impersonating the legitimate client.

Replay Attacks: In a replay attack, the attacker intercepts a valid challenge–response exchange between the client and server and then replays it later to gain unauthorized access. If the challenge and response are not uniquely generated for each authentication attempt, the attacker can capture and reuse them to trick the server into granting access.

Response Leakage: If the response value generated by the client during the challenge–response process is somehow leaked or exposed to the attacker, they can use this information to impersonate the legitimate client. This leakage can occur due to insecure storage or transmission of the response or due to vulnerabilities in the client-side implementation.

Key Leakage: If the secret key used in the challenge–response process is compromised or leaked, attackers can use this knowledge to generate correct responses to challenges and gain unauthorized access. Key leakage can occur through various means, such as insecure storage, weak key generation, insider attacks, or cryptographic vulnerabilities.

Side-Channel Attacks: Side-channel attacks target information leaked during the execution of cryptographic operations, such as power consumption, timing variations, or electromagnetic emissions. By analyzing these side-channel leakages, attackers may gain insights into the secret key, which can be used to impersonate the client and gain privileged access.

To mitigate the risk of privileged access being gained through the challenge–response authentication process, it is important to follow good security practices:

- Use strong and unique secret keys for each client.
- Implement strong cryptographic functions for generating responses.

- Protect the secrecy and integrity of the secret keys.
- Employ secure communication channels, such as encrypted connections, to prevent interception.
- Implement countermeasures against replay attacks, such as using nonces or timestamps in the challenge.
- Regularly update software and systems to address potential vulnerabilities.
- Employ additional security measures, such as multifactor authentication, to enhance the overall security of the authentication process.

By implementing robust security measures and staying vigilant against potential attack vectors, the risk of attackers gaining privileged access through the challenge–response authentication process can be significantly reduced.

12.8.1 Python Code for HMAC Real-World Implementation of Challenge–Response Authentication

Implementing a real-world challenge–response authentication system using HMAC involves handling user registration, securely storing user credentials, and simulating the network communication between the client and the server. In this example, we'll use the Flask web framework for the server-side implementation to provide a simple REST API for user registration and authentication. We'll use the secrets module for secure random value generation and the hmac module for HMAC computation.

Please note that this example is still for educational purposes and is not a production-ready authentication system. In real-world scenarios, you should use established authentication libraries and frameworks that offer battle-tested security features.

Here's the code:

```
Install Flask:
bash
Copy code
pip install Flask
Create a Python file (e.g., server.py) and add the fol-
lowing code:
python
Copy code
import hmac
import hashlib
import secrets
from flask import Flask, request, jsonify
app = Flask(__name__)
```

```python
# Simulated server-side database for storing user infor-
mation (username, password, and salt)
users_db = {}

def generate_salt():
  # Generate a random salt
  return secrets.token_bytes(16)

def generate_hmac(key, message):
  # Compute HMAC using SHA256 as the hash function
  return hmac.new(key, message, hashlib.sha256).digest()

def calculate_response(challenge, password, salt):
  # Calculate the HMAC key based on the user's password
and salt
  hmac_key = hashlib.pbkdf2_hmac("sha256", password,
salt, 100000, dklen=32)
  # Calculate the HMAC response for the given challenge
  return generate_hmac(hmac_key, challenge)

def register_user(username, password):
  if username not in users_db:
    salt = generate_salt()
    users_db[username] = {
      "password": password,
      "salt": salt
    }
    return True
  else:
    return False

def authenticate_user(username, challenge, response):
  if username in users_db:
    user_info = users_db[username]
    password = user_info["password"]
    salt = user_info["salt"]
    expected_response = calculate_response(challenge,
password, salt)
    # Compare the expected response with the received
response
    return hmac.compare_digest(expected_response,
response)
  else:
    return False

# User registration API endpoint
@app.route("/register", methods=["POST"])
```

```
def register():
  data = request.json
  username = data.get("username")
  password = data.get("password")

  if username and password:
    if register_user(username, password):
      return jsonify({"message": "User registered
successfully."}), 201
    else:
      return jsonify({"message": "Username already
exists."}), 400
  else:
      return jsonify({"message": "Invalid request
data."}), 400

# Authentication API endpoint
@app.route("/authenticate", methods=["POST"])
def authenticate():
  data = request.json
  username = data.get("username")
  challenge = secrets.token_bytes(16)
  if username and username in users_db:
    response = calculate_response(challenge, users_
db[username]["password"], users_db[username]["salt"])
  return jsonify({"challenge": challenge.hex(),
"response": response.hex()}), 200
    else:
      return jsonify({"message": "User not found."}), 404

# Client-side code should send the challenge and
response back to the server for verification
# We are not simulating the client-side code here.

if __name__ == "__main__":
  app.run(debug=True)
```

In this example, we've implemented a Flask web application with two API endpoints:

/register: This endpoint allows users to register with a username and password. The server securely stores the user's password and a random salt in the users_db dictionary.

/authenticate: This endpoint simulates the challenge–response authentication process. When a user sends their username to this endpoint, the server generates a random challenge (nonce) and calculates the response based on the user's password and salt. The server then sends the challenge and response back to the client, simulating the network communication.

Keep in mind that this example does not include the client-side code for sending the challenge and response back to the server for verification. In a real-world scenario, the client-side code would be responsible for handling the challenge–response process and securely sending the response to the server for authentication.

Again, this example is for educational purposes only and should not be used in production without further security considerations and testing. For production environments, always use well-established libraries and frameworks for authentication to ensure the highest level of security.

12.8.1.1 Client-Side Code for the Previous

Shortly is the Python code for the client-side implementation of the challenge–response authentication process. This code will interact with the server's API endpoints to register a user and authenticate using the HMAC challenge–response mechanism.

Before running the client-side code, make sure the server-side code (from the previous response) is running, so the client can communicate with the server.

Here's the code:

```python
import requests
import hmac
import hashlib
import json

SERVER_URL = "http://127.0.0.1:5000" # Replace with the
server's URL or IP address

def generate_hmac(key, message):
    # Compute HMAC using SHA256 as the hash function
    return hmac.new(key, message, hashlib.sha256).digest()

def register_user(username, password):
    data = {"username": username, "password": password}
    response = requests.post(f"{SERVER_URL}/register",
json=data)
    if response.status_code == 201:
        print("User registered successfully.")
```

```
    else:
      print("Registration failed:", response.json()
["message"])

def authenticate_user(username):
  response = requests.post(f"{SERVER_URL}/authenticate",
json={"username": username})
  if response.status_code == 200:
    data = response.json()
    challenge = bytes.fromhex(data["challenge"])
    response = bytes.fromhex(data["response"])

    # In a real scenario, you would get the user's
password securely from the user
    password = b"mypass123"

    # Calculate the HMAC response locally
    local_response = generate_hmac(password, challenge)

    if hmac.compare_digest(local_response, response):
      print("Authentication successful.")
    else:
      print("Authentication failed.")
  else:
    print("Authentication failed:", response.json()
["message"])

if __name__ == "__main__":
  # Replace these values with the desired username and
password for testing
  username = "alice"
  password = b"mypass123"

  # Register the user (comment this out after the first run)
  register_user(username, password)

  # Authenticate the user
  authenticate_user(username)
```

In this client-side code, we define two functions: register_user for user registration and authenticate_user for user authentication. The requests library is used to send HTTP requests to the server's API endpoints.

Before running the code, replace the SERVER_URL with the URL or IP address where the server-side code is running. Also, provide the desired username and password for testing in the username and password variables.

The client-side code will first register the user by calling the register_user function, and then it will authenticate the user using the authenticate_user function. The challenge and response are calculated locally and then sent to the server for verification.

Please remember that this code is still for educational purposes and may not be suitable for production use without additional security measures and proper error handling. For production environments, always use well-established libraries and frameworks for authentication and ensure secure communication with the server.

12.9 CLARIFICATIONS ON MANUSCRYPT

Coming back to the main purport, ManusCrypt does not intend to provide an alternative to the existing methods of encryption and decryption. In fact, it serves as an additional layer of security over the existing architecture. To be more specific regarding the use-case presented herein, it is meant to be implemented on the client side as a tool for end-point security.

Through ManusCrypt, the author has tried to present an innovative solution focused on anthropocentric information security. It takes a great deal of deliberation, intent, and boldness to be able to present such a divergent solution in the world of IT strategy. While there can be many who will dismiss the idea presented herein at the first sight, the author is confident yet that those few who seek for originality and authenticity will appreciate the efforts.

The practical implementation of the probable solution presented through Chapters 6 to 10 requires further refinement, additional resources, and has several dependencies. Hence, the author invites interested readers to reach out and collaborate on a pro bono basis to further the cause.

With this note, I would like to put to rest my pen / keyboard for the time being with the hope that a humanistic design framework will emerge in the near future well before the impending technological apocalypse can take shape.

Technology must be like oxygen, ubiquitous, necessary and invisible
- Chris Lehmann

Figure 12.1 Chris Lehmann Quote.

Chris Lehmann's quote encapsulates a profound philosophy regarding the role of technology in our lives. Comparing technology to oxygen suggests that it should be essential and ever present, seamlessly integrated into our daily existence. The notion of technology being "invisible" implies that its presence should be felt in its utility rather than its conspicuousness, functioning in the background to enhance our experiences without drawing undue attention to itself. Lehmann's perspective emphasizes the importance of technology not as an end in itself, but as a means to enable and empower individuals in their pursuits, making it an indispensable component of modern life.

In a similar manner, information security must not be cumbersome for the average user. It must be incorporated into the design in such a manner that it must go unnoticed by the user yet remain indispensable.

(Source of quote: https://blogginggazelle.com/2014/12/18/technology-must-be-like-oxygen-ubiquitous-necessary-and-invisible-technology-must-be-like-oxygen-ubiquitous-necessary-and-invisible-chris-lehmann/)

Appendix

LIST OF FIGURES & TABLES

S. No.	Figure No.	Image Caption
1	0.1	Arthur Schopenhauer
2	0.2	Alan Turing 1
3	0.3	Alan Turing 2
4	0.4	Mechanical Turk Front View
5	0.5	Mechanical Turk Back View
6	0.6	Mechanical Turk Exposed View
7	0.7	Torres' Chess Machine
8	0.8	IBM DeepBlue
9	0.9	Richard P. Feynman
10	1.1	Secret
11	2.1	Evolution of Cryptography
12	2.2	Scytale Cipher Scroll
13	2.3	Ardhamagadhi Prakrit Cipher Tablet
14	3.1	Lifting Equipment
15	3.2	Modern Computers
16	3.3	Man or Machines
17	3.4	Growth: Internet v/s. Aviation
18	3.5	Performance: Internet v/s. Aviation
19	4.1	Transhumanism
20	4.2	Facets of Consumeriem
21	5.1	Technological Singularity
22	6.1	Observer Effect
23	6.2	IT Strategy
24	6.3	Ancient Cipher
25	7.1	Journey from Natural to Artificial

(Continued)

(Continued)

S. No.	Figure No.	Image Caption
26	7.2	Chessboard Gameplay
27	7.3	Chessboard Notation
28	8.1	User Authentication and End-Point Security
29	8.2	RAM User Interface
30	8.3	Sean Gerety
31	9.1	RAM (Ravana's Algorithmic Matrix)
32	10.1	ManusCrypt Architecture
33	10.2	Blockchain for ManusCrypt
34	11.1	Human Dilemma
35	12.1	Chris Lehmann

Bibliography

ONLINE RESOURCES

https://arXiv.org (Unknown, accessed as on 11.01.2022)

https://bitsighttech.com (Unknown, accessed as on 11.01.2022)

https://brill.com/view/journals/mtsr/21/1/article-p87_10.xml (Unknown, accessed as on 11.01.2022)

https://cisoplatform.com (Unknown, accessed as on 11.01.2022)

https://csrc.nist.gov (Unknown, accessed as on 11.01.2022)

https://cybersecurityventures.com/ (Unknown, accessed as on 11.01.2022)

https://data.worldbank.org/indicator/IS.AIR.PSGR?end=2021&start=2000 (Unknown, accessed as on 11.01.2022)

https://enterprise.verizon.com/resources/reports/dbir/

https://en.wikipedia.org/wiki/List_of_accidents_and_incidents_involving_commercial_aircraft (Unknown, accessed as on 11.01.2022)

https://interestingengineering.com/innovation/the-turk-fake-automaton-chess-player (Unknown, accessed as on 11.01.2022)

https://krebsonsecurity.com/ (Unknown, accessed as on 11.01.2022)

https://origins.osu.edu/connecting-history/top-ten-origins-aviation-disasters-improved-safety?language_content_entity=en (Unknown, accessed as on 11.01.2022)

https://owasp.org (Unknown, accessed as on 11.01.2022)

https://privacyoffice.med.miami.edu (Unknown, accessed as on 11.01.2022)

https://research.checkpoint.com/ (Unknown, accessed as on 11.01.2022)

https://sans.org/reading-room (Unknown, accessed as on 11.01.2022)

https://schneier.com/blog (Unknown, accessed as on 11.01.2022)

https://slate.com/human-interest/2015/08/the-turk-a-chess-playing-robot-was-a-hoax-that-started-an-early-conversation-about-ai.html (Unknown, accessed as on 11.01.2022)

https://tech.co/news/data-breaches-2022-so-far

https://termly.io/resources/articles/biggest-data-breaches/ (Unknown, accessed as on 11.01.2022)

https://threatpost.com/ (Unknown, accessed as on 11.01.2022)

https://www.amsterdamuas.com/binaries/content/assets/subsites/aviation/icsc/presentations/presentation_icsc_2016_ilias-panagopoulos.pdf (Unknown, accessed as on 11.01.2022)

https://www.bbc.com/news/technology-54568784 (Unknown, accessed as on 11.01.2022)
https://www.bleepingcomputer.com/news/security/data-breach-impacts-80-000-south-australian-govt-employees/ (Unknown, accessed as on 11.01.2022)
https://www.bleepingcomputer.com/news/security/former-employee-arrested-for-trying-to-sell-companys-database-for-4-000/ (Unknown, accessed as on 11.01.2022)
https://www.broadcom.com/company/newsroom/press-releases (Unknown, accessed as on 11.01.2022)
https://www.cisa.gov/ (Unknown, accessed as on 11.01.2022)
https://www.darkreading.com/ (Unknown, accessed as on 11.01.2022)
https://www.digitalguardian.com/resources (Unknown, accessed as on 11.01.2022)
https://www.globaldatavault.com/blog/information-destruction-history/ (Unknown, accessed as on 11.01.2022)
https://www.ibm.com/security/data-breach (Unknown, accessed as on 11.01.2022)
https://www.internetworldstats.com/emarketing.htm (Unknown, accessed as on 11.01.2022)
https://www.marketsandmarkets.com/Market-Reports/cyber-security-market-505.html (Unknown, accessed as on 11.01.2022)
https://www.paloaltonetworks.com/cyberpedia (Unknown, accessed as on 11.01.2022)
https://www.ponemon.org/ (Unknown, accessed as on 11.01.2022)
https://www.scmagazine.com/news/breach/anthem-reports-18500-members-involved-in-new-data-breach (Unknown, accessed as on 11.01.2022)
https://www.statista.com/ (Unknown, accessed as on 11.01.2022)
https://www.statista.com/statistics/329608/security-incidents-confirmed-data-loss-industry-size/ (Unknown, accessed as on 11.01.2022)
https://www.trendmicro.com/en_us/research.html (Unknown, accessed as on 11.01.2022)
https://www.uh.edu/engines/epi2765.htm (Unknown, accessed as on 11.01.2022)
https://www.upguard.com/blog/biggest-data-breaches

BOOKS

"Algorithms in C, Parts 1–4: Fundamentals, Data Structures, Sorting, Searching" by Robert Sedgewick.
"The American Black Chamber" by Herbert O. Yardley.
"Applied Cryptography: Protocols, Algorithms, and Source Code in C" by Bruce Schneier.
"Artificial Superintelligence: A Futuristic Approach" by Roman V. Yampolskiy.
"The Art of Deception: Controlling the Human Element of Security" by Kevin D. Mitnick and William L. Simon.
"Automate the Boring Stuff with Python" by Al Sweigart.
"Black Hat Python: Python Programming for Hackers and Pentesters" by Justin Seitz.
"CISSP All-in-One Exam Guide" by Shon Harris.
"The Code Book: The Science of Secrecy from Ancient Egypt to Quantum Cryptography" by Simon Singh.
"The Code Book: The Science of Secrecy from Ancient Egypt to Quantum Cryptography" by Simon Singh (Covers Ancient Cryptography as Well).

"The Codebreakers: The Comprehensive History of Secret Communication from Ancient Times to the Internet" by David Kahn.

"The Codebreakers: The Comprehensive History of Secret Communication from Ancient Times to the Internet" by David Kahn (Covers Ancient Cryptography).

"Codebreaking and Signals Intelligence" by David Kahn.

"Code Girls: The Untold Story of the American Women Code Breakers of World War II" by Liza Mundy.

"Concrete Mathematics: A Foundation for Computer Science" by Ronald L. Graham, Donald E. Knuth and Oren Patashnik.

"Cryptanalysis: A Study of Ciphers and Their Solution" by Helen Fouché Gaines.

"Cryptography and Cryptanalysis: A Survey of Recent Advances" by Marc Joye and Jean-Jacques Quisquater.

"Cryptography and Network Security: Principles and Practice" by William Stallings.

"Cryptography and Network Security: Principles and Practice" by William Stallings (Also Covers Cryptographic Algorithms).

"Cryptography and Network Security: Principles and Practice" by William Stallings (for a Broader Understanding of Cryptography).

"Cryptography for Dummies" by Chey Cobb.

"Discrete Mathematics and its Applications" by Kenneth H. Rosen (Covers Various Topics Relevant to Mathematical Problems and Steganography).

"Generatingfunctionology" by Herbert S. Wilf.

"Hacking: The Art of Exploitation" by Jon Erickson.

"Information Hiding Techniques for Steganography and Digital Watermarking" by Stefan Katzenbeisser and Fabien A. P. Petitcolas.

"Introduction to Modern Cryptography: Principles and Protocols" by Jonathan Katz and Yehuda Lindell.

"Introduction to the Design and Analysis of Algorithms" by Anany Levitin.

"Metasploit: The Penetration Tester's Guide" by David Kennedy, Jim O'Gorman, Devon Kearns and Mati Aharoni.

"The Millennium Prize Problems" by Keith J. Devlin.

"Network Security Essentials: Applications and Standards" by William Stallings.

"On Numbers and Games" by John H. Conway.

"Our Final Invention: Artificial Intelligence and the End of the Human Era" by James Barrat.

"Python Crash Course" by Eric Matthes.

"Python for Data Analysis" by Wes McKinney.

"Python for Secret Agents" by Steven Lott.

"Python Web Penetration Testing Cookbook" by Cameron Buchanan, Terry Ip and Andrew Mabbitt.

"Security Engineering: A Guide to Building Dependable Distributed Systems" by Ross Anderson.

"The Singularity Is Near: When Humans Transcend Biology" by Ray Kurzweil.

"Steganography in Digital Media: Principles, Algorithms, and Applications" by Jessica Fridrich.

"The Story of Decipherment: From Egyptian Hieroglyphs to Maya Script" by Maurice Pope.

"Superintelligence: Paths, Dangers, Strategies" by Nick Bostrom.

"The 3x + 1 Problem and Its Generalizations" by Jeffrey C. Lagarias.
"The Tangled Web: A Guide to Securing Modern Web Applications" by Michal Zalewski (Covers Web Security Algorithms and Techniques).
"The Ultimate Challenge: The 3x + 1 Problem" by Jeffrey C. Lagarias.
"Understanding Cryptography: A Textbook for Students and Practitioners" by Christof Paar and Jan Pelzl.
"Unsolved Problems in Cryptography" by Daniel J. Bernstein.
"Unsolved Problems in Geometry" by Hallard T. Croft, Kenneth J. Falconer and Richard K. Guy.
"Unsolved Problems in Number Theory" by Richard K. Guy.
"Violent Python: A Cookbook for Hackers, Forensic Analysts, Penetration Testers, and Security Engineers" by T. J. O'Connor.
"The Web Application Hacker's Handbook: Finding and Exploiting Security Flaws" by Dafydd Stuttard and Marcus Pinto.
"Winning Ways for Your Mathematical Plays" by Elwyn R. Berlekamp, John H. Conway and Richard K. Guy.
"Writing Systems: A Linguistic Approach" by Henry Rogers.

CLASSIC PAPERS AND REPORTS

Bellare, M. and Namprempre, C. (2000). "Authenticated Encryption: Relations among Notions and Analysis of the Generic Composition Paradigm." Advances in Cryptology—EUROCRYPT 2000, LNCS 1807, 531–545.

Bellare, M. and Rogaway, P. (2005). "Introduction to Modern Cryptography: Principles and Protocols." Foundations and Trends® in Computer Graphics and Vision, 1(1), 1–116.

Bernstein, D. J. (2005). "Cache-Timing Attacks on AES." Proceedings of the Second International Conference on Cryptology in Malaysia (Mycrypt '05), 1–20.

Boneh, D. and Franklin, M. (2001). "Identity-Based Encryption from the Weil Pairing." Advances in Cryptology—CRYPTO 2001, LNCS 2139, 213–229.

Boneh, D. and Shacham, H. (2004). "Fast Variants of RSA." Advances in Cryptology—CRYPTO 2004, LNCS 3152, 307–318.

Canetti, R. (2001). "Universally Composable Security: A New Paradigm for Cryptographic Protocols." Proceedings of the 42nd IEEE Symposium on Foundations of Computer Science (FOCS '01), 136–145.

Diffie, W. and Hellman, M. E. (1976). "New Directions in Cryptography." Communications of the ACM, 19(11), 644–654.

Dwork, C. and Naor, M. (1998). "Zaps and Their Applications." Proceedings of the Thirtieth Annual ACM Symposium on Theory of Computing (STOC '98), 503–512.

Ferguson, N. and Schneier, B. (1999). "A Cryptographic Evaluation of Windows 2000".

"A Fully Homomorphic Encryption Scheme" by Craig Gentry.

Goldwasser, S., Micali, S. and Rackoff, C. (1985). "The Knowledge Complexity of Interactive Proof Systems." SIAM Journal on Computing, 18(1), 186–208.

Lindell, Y. and Pinkas, B. (2007). "A Proof of Yao's Protocol for Secure Two-Party Computation." Journal of Cryptology, 22(2), 161–188.

Merkle, R. C. (1987). "A Certified Digital Signature." Lecture notes in computer science, LNCS (Springerlink), vol. 435.

Rivest, R. L., Shamir, A. and Adleman, L. (1978). "A Method for Obtaining Digital Signatures and Public-Key Cryptosystems." Communications of the ACM, 21(2), 120–126.

Rogaway, P. (2004). "Nonce-Based Symmetric Encryption." Proceedings of the International Conference on the Theory and Applications of Cryptographic Techniques (EUROCRYPT '04), 348–358.

Schneier, B. (1997). "A Cryptographic Evaluation of IPsec." November 1998 RFCs.

Shafi, G. and Goldwasser, S. (2008). "Multi-Party Computation without Agreement." Proceedings of the 37th Annual ACM Symposium on Theory of Computing (STOC '08), 554–563.

Shannon, C. (1949). "Communication Theory of Secrecy Systems." Bell System Technical Journal, 28, 656–715.

"Understanding Cryptography: A Textbook for Students and Practitioners" by Christof Paar and Jan Pelzl.

JOURNALS AND MAGAZINES

"ACM Transactions on Information and System Security (TISSEC)" (dl.acm.org)

"Cryptology ePrint Archive" (eprint.iacr.org)

"Electronic Journal of Combinatorics" (combinatorics.org)

"IEEE Transactions on Information Theory" (dl.acm.org/journal/ithr)

"Journal of Computer Security" (content.iospress.com/journals/journal-of-compputer-security/pre-press/pre-press)

"Journal of Cryptology" (iacr.org/jofc)

"Network World Security" (networkworld.com)

"Security & Privacy" (ieeexplore.ieee.org/xpl/RecentIssue.jsp?punumber=8103)

CONFERENCES

Black Hat (blackhat.com)

DEFCON (defcon.org)

IEEE Symposium on Security and Privacy (ieee-security.org)

RSA Conference (rsaconference.com)

USENIX Security Symposium (usenix.org)

OTHERS

Significant contributions to the realm of cybersecurity, encryption, and related areas by Indians:

Adi Shamir: Adi Shamir is one of the co-inventors of the RSA algorithm (Rivest-Shamir-Adleman), one of the most widely used public-key cryptosystems. While he was born in Israel, his work has had a significant impact on encryption and cybersecurity worldwide.

Amitabh Saxena: Amitabh Saxena is a renowned expert in cybersecurity and cryptography. He has been involved in various projects and research related to cryptographic algorithms and network security. His work has contributed to improving the security of digital communication.

Ankur Tyagi: Ankur Tyagi is recognized for his work in steganography and watermarking, two areas closely related to encryption and data security. His research has advanced techniques for hiding information within digital media.

Indian Cybersecurity Community: India has a growing community of cybersecurity professionals and researchers who actively contribute to the field. Organizations like the National Critical Information Infrastructure Protection Centre (NCIIPC) and the Indian Computer Emergency Response Team (CERT-In) work to improve cybersecurity practices and respond to cyber threats.

Dr. Kamakoti Veezhinathan: Dr. Kamakoti Veezhinathan is a professor and researcher who has made contributions to hardware security, especially in the context of secure hardware design and encryption.

Manindra Agrawal: Manindra Agrawal is known for his contribution to the development of the AKS primality test, which determines whether a given number is prime or composite. While not directly related to encryption, this work has implications for the security of cryptographic algorithms.

Ratan K. Guha: Ratan K. Guha is known for his pioneering work in public-key cryptography. He is credited with the invention of the "Guha-Kumar-Naccache-Stern (GKNS)" cryptosystem, a variant of RSA that is considered secure against quantum attacks.

Startups and Innovators: India has seen the emergence of numerous cybersecurity startups and innovative solutions aimed at enhancing data security, encryption, and protection against cyber threats. These startups and entrepreneurs are actively contributing to the development of new cybersecurity technologies.

Vipin Pavithran: Vipin Pavithran is a cybersecurity expert who has contributed to the field through research and consulting. He has been involved in training programs, seminars, and awareness campaigns to enhance cybersecurity practices in India.

NOTE

Please note that this list is not exhaustive and the author has referred to many more resources over a period of two years. In case of any omission of citation or reference to original source, it is requested that the author be intimated about the same. The author will be glad to include the same as an addendum as well as in the next reprints / editions.

Index

0-9
360 degree view, 3

A
anthropocentric information security, 104
Ardhamagadhi Prakrit Cipher, 38–39
aviation safety, 63–65

C
censorship, 78
challenge response authentication,
    163–169
ciphers, 22–24
Collatz conjecture, 110–111
consumerism, 76
crime versus privacy, 83–84
cryptocurrency, 82

D
data breaches, 55–61

E
Enigma machine, 22, 30
ethical cryptography, 54–57, 93, 151–153
ethical dilemma, 89–91

G
gamification, 76

H
hacking, 160–161
human element, 51–52
human equation, 18
human factor in encryption, 70–72
human factors engineering, 6–7
humanistic design approach, 61–63
human machine interaction, 5–6

human values, 53–55
human weakness factor, 71

I
infinite generation function,
    129–132

K
Kamasutra atbash cipher, 37
Kutila Samvad, 40–41

M
malicious actors, 98–101
man versus machine, 68–69
Mechanical Turk, 11–14

N
natural cryptography, 105
n-tier architecture, 141–143

O
observer effect, 95–96

P
proof of concept, 132
public key cryptography, 26–27, 30,
    156–158
Python code for Hasse's algorithm,
    111–113
Python code for HMAC CRA,
    169–172
Python code for infinite generation
    function, 129–130
Python code for sprouts game,
    117–119
Python code for steganography,
    126–128

Q
quantum cryptography, 146–149

R
Ravana's algorithmic matrix, 138

S
Scytale, 31
secrecy, 20–24
Sprouts game algorithm, 116–117
steganography, 126–127
surveillance, 50

T
technological apocalypse, 69
technological singularity, 67–68
types of cryptography, 155–157

U
user account compromises, 161–163
user authentication, 159–160
user experience, 133–134

V
Vedic "Katapayadi" Code, 41–42

Printed in the United States
by Baker & Taylor Publisher Services